CW00794523

light
movement
embrace

Houses in the Sun

house + house

light
movement
embrace

Houses in the Sun

cathi & steven house

Published in Australia in 2008 by
The Images Publishing Group Pty Ltd
ABN 89 059 734 431
6 Bastow Place, Mulgrave, Victoria 3170, Australia
Tel: +61 3 9561 5544 Fax: +61 3 9561 4860
books@imagespublishing.com
www.imagespublishing.com

Copyright © The Images Publishing Group Pty Ltd 2008
The Images Publishing Group Reference Number: 790

National Library of Australia Cataloguing-in-Publication entry:

Author: House, Steven, 1952–

Title: Houses in the sun : light movement embrace / Steven House ;
             Cathi House.

ISBN: 978 1 86470 239 2 (hbk.)

Subjects: House, Steven, 1952–
             House, Cathi, 1953–
             Architects—United States
             Architecture, Domestic—United States
             Architecture—United States—20th century

Other Authors/Contributors:
             House, Cathi, 1953–

Dewey Number:
             728.370973

Edited by Beth Browne

Designed by Steven and Cathi House

Digital production by The Graphic Image Studio Pty Ltd, Australia
www.tgis.com.au

Pre-publishing services by Splitting Image Colour Studio Pty Ltd, Australia
Printed by Paramount Printing Company Limited, Hong Kong

IMAGES has included on its website a page for special notices in relation
to this and its other publications. Please visit www.imagespublishing.com.

Contents

6   Handcrafted Modernism
by Steven D. Lavine

8   A Journey into Spatial Thinking
by D. Eugene Egger

10   The Process of Design
by Cathi and Steven House

14   Dos Iguanas

34   Calle Paloma

50   Anderson Valley

64   Casa Estrellas

80   Harris Place

90   Casa de Buenas Almas

100   Butternut

120   Teaberry Lane

130   Casa Joya

142   Sleepy Hollow

160   Parrot Tree Plantation

174   Moraquita

184   Casa Renacimiento

208   Southdown Court

220   Ridgecrest

232   Francisco Marquez

242   Coral Sands

252   Golden Gate

260   Rincon Ridge

270   Palo Colorado

282   Engaging the Human Spirit
by Philip Enquist

284   Light Movement Embrace
by Cathi House

292   Firm Profile

293   Selected Bibliography

294   Project Credits

296   Acknowledgments

Handcrafted Modernism

By Steven D. Lavine

I was first introduced to Cathi and Steven House in San Miguel de Allende, Mexico, which, along with the San Francisco Bay Area, has become one of the centers of their architectural practice. San Miguel is home to a substantial émigré community, which struggles, not always successfully, to combine modern amenity with respect for traditional Mexican building styles. On entering the Houses' San Miguel home for the first time, I was struck at once with the seamless merging of tradition and contemporary practice. Built around a central courtyard in the tradition of both Mediterranean and Mexican homes, with the bold use of color associated with such Mexican modernists as Luis Barragán and Ricardo Legoretta, the thick adobe wall at the street gave way unobtrusively to sculpted, light-filled spaces. Beyond the arch of the entry vestibule, one encounters the crisp geometry of a dark-hued, stepped concrete balustrade set against a lighter colored wall punctured with a small, perfectly square window, which is the same scale as the old, textured square pavers on which the ensemble rests. Here, as throughout the house, there is a comfortable mix of historically derived materials such as stone and wood, with the contemporary inflection given, for example, by the steel-framed gridded wall of glass that joins the living room to the irregularly shaped central courtyard. Rooms on multiple levels open onto the courtyard, offering glimpses that call on the visitor to explore. Though the footprint is modest in the case of their home, the house seems curiously large because of the complex geometries and the multiple levels joined by cleverly deployed staircases that can function as events in themselves. And everywhere, light: entering boldly from the courtyard as well as more subtly from hidden skylights and eclectic light fixtures—in any given room entering from multiple angles and constantly changing as the day passes.

As I've since learned, the Houses' home in San Miguel offers a microcosm for all of their work. First, there is attention to place and to the elements associated with a particular locale. Their homes, even when grand, always seem to belong, not in a slavish way for never are the Houses merely imitative, but because they join local building techniques with more general historical precedent (often deriving from the Mediterranean, which shares a climate with their San Francisco home base) and a clean, upright, well-lit modernity.

Their homes array themselves logically around central courtyards or gardens, the rooms offering privacy and yet connected to one another in ways that draw the eye with the promise of delights to come. Staircases and hallways function actively, sometimes leading one forward along a curve or switchback, almost as in the narrow streets and walkways of an Italian hill town. The materiality of these houses matters deeply. Stone, wood, concrete, and diverse metals, often used in contrasting ways, offer the safety of the solidly built, while giving pleasure to the eye and touch.

Enclosed in ways that are comfortingly secure, their houses simultaneously open themselves outward in a trusting way, through the height and frequently emphasized verticality of their rooms, through their confident contemporaneity, and, most importantly, through the easy passage of room to room and inside to outside. The people who live here—these houses seem to say—have the internal sense of self necessary to be alone and the familial and civic sense that makes them want to join with others.

In their humane and handcrafted modernism, with its deep sense of human comfort and pleasure and its inheritance from Mediterranean domestic architecture, Steven and Cathi House carry forward the tradition of Bernard Rudofsky, noted architect, writer, social historian, educator, and traveler. Educated at the Bauhaus-influenced Virginia Tech School of Architecture, the Houses were taught architecture in the context of general principles of design and also encouraged to explore painting, photography, and ceramics. After graduating and at a time when they did not yet know Rudofsky's work, they traveled in the Mediterranean and lived for a time on the Greek Island of Santorini as Rudofsky had forty-six years before them. Like Rudofsky, this experience affected them deeply, clearly helping to shape their professional lives. Later they came to know Rudofsky personally, corresponding with him until his death in 1988. Their beautiful meditation on vernacular architecture and town forms in their 2004 volume— *Mediterranean Villages: An Architectural Journey*—is in the tradition of Rudofsky's drawings and watercolors and particularly his groundbreaking exhibition and book, *Architecture without Architects*. The Houses record their impressions of villages in Italy, Greece, Dalmatia, and Spain in photographs and drawings: the

secure movement from the enclosed to open space, the staircase as pathway, the dazzling power of light and shadow, the pleasures of irregularity and the human touch.

Carrying forward the modernist questioning of the fundamental premises of architecture, the Houses arrive, as Rudofsky did, not in the universalist minimalism of Walter Gropius and of Le Corbusier's *machine á habiter* and not in a maximalist assertion of modern engineering's ability to create any form the architect can imagine, but by embracing what the Mediterranean vernacular had to teach about sensuous enjoyment and human dignity. This dignity is achieved in a life lived both privately and in conjunction with others, in the infinitude and wonder of shifting light and hand-wrought detail and in the clarity and interconnection of built forms. What more could one ask of home than that it combine security with wonder, all the while fortifying what is most personal and most communal in our lives. I've not lived in a home designed by Cathi and Steven, though even as I write they are renovating the home my wife, Janet Sternburg, and I own in San Miguel de Allende, but I have experienced the at-once-comforting and fortifying influence of their houses and I have a hunch that living in one is going to be a great gift.

Steven D. Lavine, President
California Institute of the Arts

A Journey into Spatial Thinking

By D. Eugene Egger

I would ask the fortunate guest to this book's visual feast to undertake the formidable challenge of carefully considering the behind-appearance design processes cultivated by Cathi and Steven House. Relationships with clients, program demands, building methods, site, and material culture from around the world rigorously inform their design decisions. The works presented here exhibit close ties to the land, client ownership of ideas, and skillfully designed common ground between necessarily independent parts. House + House architecture evolves from the human condition that inhabits it.

Resisting stylistic preconceptions, the House + House practice of architecture begins not with solutions to design challenges but with patient, sensitive, and disciplined probing of implicit, flowing streams of thought inhabiting the design environment. Thoughtful interviews with clients are carefully documented as parallel visual/spatial habitable accommodations. These project journals not only embrace the specific design problem at hand but also bring to light new consequences of combining often-isolated fragments of client desires and needs. Continuous design dialogue with their clients allows House + House to produce multiple design proposals that strive to maintain and enhance the ambient agreement of dwelling well in harmony with particular functional demands.

As an architect and educator for four decades, I have witnessed first-hand the tenuous demands necessary to intelligently inform one's critical design decisions. Nurturing a continuous design inquiry with a client must be predicated upon building together a sustained, collective learning environment for productive creative thought. Schools of Architecture seek this environment, but few are able to sustain it through professional pressures of prescribed production and mechanistic metrics of success.

Cathi and Steven have carried and developed a cornerstone from their formal education for over 30 years. Knowing them since their early years in the College of Architecture at Virginia Tech, I recall fondly having the privilege of directing an Architecture Study Abroad Program in the early 1970s where Steven, sitting atop the outer city wall of Dubrovnik, spontaneously proclaimed for all to hear that he had just discovered a way to sketch the presence of a place. Steven's simple realization confirmed for me a Virginia Tech maxim that design abilities can be acquired and maintained when the design process is simultaneously understood as discovery and as instrumental problem solving. The design process is equally as important as the final product. Discovery through design expands boundaries of problem solving.

This special client–architect dialogue nurtured by House + House can be illuminated by the idea of "high and low context cultures" popularized and developed by anthropologist Edward T. Hall throughout his work, but specifically in his 1976 book *Beyond Culture*. He has always sought to learn from significantly different ways of communication exhibited by different cultures. Participatory design processes between architects and users must function in a climate of trust, instilled traditions, and shared standards of quality—a "high-context culture," according to Hall. It must become a like-minded meeting, carefully crafted and sustained by the mutual benefits of a new clarity to previously ill-defined problems. The designer thinks spatially, with the means to build habitable places proposed verbally by the user. A high-context culture is particularly receptive to outcomes produced by new combinations of commonly known elements.

Cathi and Steven literally grow their projects from the seeds of their clients' circumstances and nurture these gardens of delight with their own remarkably perceptive findings from extensive travels through many lands and ages. To more fully appreciate the depth of their sensibilities to works borne from cultural heritage, one must know their important book, *Mediterranean Villages: An Architectural Journey* (2004)—composed of over 300 folio-size pages of graphic explorations into ancient living habitats throughout Italy, Greece, Dalmatia, and Spain. This record of their travels and insights, in haunting photographs and personal ink sketches, testifies to a rare, disciplined skill to present architecture that carries memory, duration, and material presence. Indigenous architecture, made one with nature, seamless between functions and readable as single entities, has been their constant focus of study.

Giving contemporary contours to ancient habitats is a very difficult leap of imagination and design skill. Finding and translating the web of significant relationships imbedded in ways of dwelling is the primary aim of House + House's unique design dialogue with clients and their building sites. Avoiding nostalgic replication of borrowed vernacular forms from other cultures, Cathi and Steven manage to maintain the critical ideas discovered through their travels and to create authentic, pluralistic settlement patterns for contemporary living. In Jean Cocteau's 1926 *Call to Order* he declares his modernist preference for ideas versus dragging forms from the past: "Beethoven is irksome in his developments, but not Bach, because Beethoven develops the form and Bach, the idea."

The extreme rarity of design skill to give new form to enduring ideas recalls the valuable lesson that Le Corbusier outlines in his 1920s travel journals where he marvels at Hadrian's ability to realize, in then-contemporary Roman building language, ideas found throughout the vast, diverse 4th-century Roman Empire. Villa Adriana, east of Rome, displays an excavated 300-acre collection of transplanted architectural ideas, re-designed and ordered by the topography of the land rather than by preconceived Classical configurations. The necessity for deep-rooted, inherent references secures memory for timeless reunions.

House + House projects take on the deep-rooted indigenous village character. Employing those qualities makes them one with nature, seamless between functions and readable as single entities full of new material culture and a "tangible spirit" unique to the individual client and the land.

Cathi and Steven think with infused spatial color, inclusive boundaries, and sculpted natural light. Their ability to grasp qualities that seemingly different things share yields habitable, continuous environments, where the passage to places is as important as the arrival. Hallways are village streets forecasting anticipated functions. Vivid color fills one's memory of the garden. And pragmatic building elements—walls, doors, stairs, windows, balconies, and columns—are figures sharing the space with human occupants creating gentle family gatherings in an architecture of closeness at many scales.

The work of House + House can be compared to an imagined, youthful Luis Barragán, where serenity is respectfully colored with playful honesty. It was inevitable that Cathi and Steven embraced Mexico as their second home. Dividing their time between San Miguel de Allende, Mexico, and San Francisco, they surround themselves with color and culture permanently marked by time's design processes.

To fortify oneself against tendencies to build one-dimensional, linear habitations that ignore the inexhaustible resources often hidden within the land and the lives of its inhabitants, students, clients, and professionals alike should closely study *Houses in the Sun: Light, Movement, Embrace,* built work that critically reveals its content and its sources.

D. Eugene Egger, Professor of Architecture
Virginia Tech

The Process of Design

By Cathi and Steven House

At the start of each project we use a simple poem by David Whyte to begin the design process—to help clarify what it is we and our clients are doing together: "We shape ourselves to fit this world and by the world are shaped again, the visible and the invisible working together in common cause to produce the miraculous. So may we, in this life, trust to those elements we have yet to imagine, and look for the shape of our own true self, by forming it well to the great intangibles about us." A great deal of trust is necessary in the making of a building. Our clients must trust in themselves and in us. We, in turn, must trust ourselves and our process, for it is true that together we make decisions that shape lives based on the invisible and great intangibles.

There are really three parties to this design process—the land, the client, and the architect—each party equal and the chemistry between them unique. Every piece of land will communicate what is appropriate to be built on it; how the sun, moon, and stars sweep across it, how breezes caress it, how the fragrance from nearby gardens touches it, alignments to neighbors, views, and vegetation. Each client is different from every other—their needs, their dreams, their family dynamics and social interactions—and to ignore their unique characteristics would be a loss, not only for them, but also for us. The pleasure of coming to know each client personally, at a level they did not expect, has been one of our rewards in designing homes. Learning who they are is an adventure of discovery. And every architect is different from every other, how they work, who they are, their history, education, experience, and what they bring to the mix that may be unique. It is the chemistry between these parties working in common cause, that shapes the world, forming it well to those elements that have yet to be imagined.

Each new project is a journey that begins when life changes and a family develops new needs for their home. Most people are too busy to search beyond their immediate needs, and the frustrations that bring them to an architect are pressing. Their program is usually developed in response to the inadequacies of their current home. Their lives have changed, and this pressure for change comes with fear and worry. Large sums of money are involved, many decisions must be made about things they may not have experienced, and they must commit to these decisions after seeing only representations—diagrams, drawings, models, photos—a sink, a faucet, a refrigerator—all disembodied in showrooms. But they also have a unique opportunity—they can decide to just solve their need, or they can expand the opportunity to explore new possibilities. This is where hope comes into the equation. Hope touches into parts of who they are, or could be, that often get set aside for reasons of practicality or budget or a sense of being beyond reach.

As we begin the design process, we start with a thorough site analysis, then careful explorations into alternative arrangements of the particular building elements on the land, analyzing the pros and cons of each arrangement. Our initial diagrams are simple, illustrating for our clients what their options are and inviting them to speculate about directions they may not have considered. The diagrams also help our clients become comfortable reading plans as they will ultimately make hundreds of choices based on a medium that is unfamiliar to most. Our drawings always seek to orient, with furniture and windows appearing even in the most rudimentary diagrams, so that there is a level of confidence as decisions are made.

Initial Sketches

To illustrate our initial design process we have chosen a project for a new home on a dense urban site in San Miguel de Allende, Mexico. In the 465 years since the founding of this town, a combination of wars, political upheavals, and the strife and beauty of a rich history and varied culture have re-shaped the land, leaving this unusually shaped piece—the remainder after portions of a larger whole had been divided for generations, given to sons and grandsons. A narrow entrance from a principal street, four blocks from the central square, leads past a series of rooms and shacks, an abandoned stairway, and up a slope to flat land with a few trees and a broad view to the west, overlooking the town's historic center with myriad church towers and domes. The clients are an American couple retiring to a new life in Mexico with their dog, and their program includes living room, dining room, kitchen, office/studio, and three bedrooms and bathrooms, all woven into gardens and terraces. The temperate climate allows the possibility of rooms connected through exterior spaces.

1 Site analysis showing sun orientation and shade, primary and secondary views, neighbors' windows, existing topography, and vegetation. 2–3 Diagrammatic studies of potential positions for primary spaces in response to the answers in the clients' questionnaires. 4–5 Alignment analysis illustrating elemental forms and how they might touch, overlap, and align. 6–7 Conceptual bubble diagrams showing potential relationships between spaces and land with thoughts on connections and views. 8–15 Furniture and gardens are added to the diagrams for scale and clarity in exploring various room and courtyard layouts. 16–18 Circulation diagrams study potential movement through the land, physically and visually. 19–20 Studies of how circulation might affect the shapes and sizes of the rooms. 22–25 A series of potential alternative plans developed in direct response to the questionnaire, the site analysis, and the diagrammatic studies.

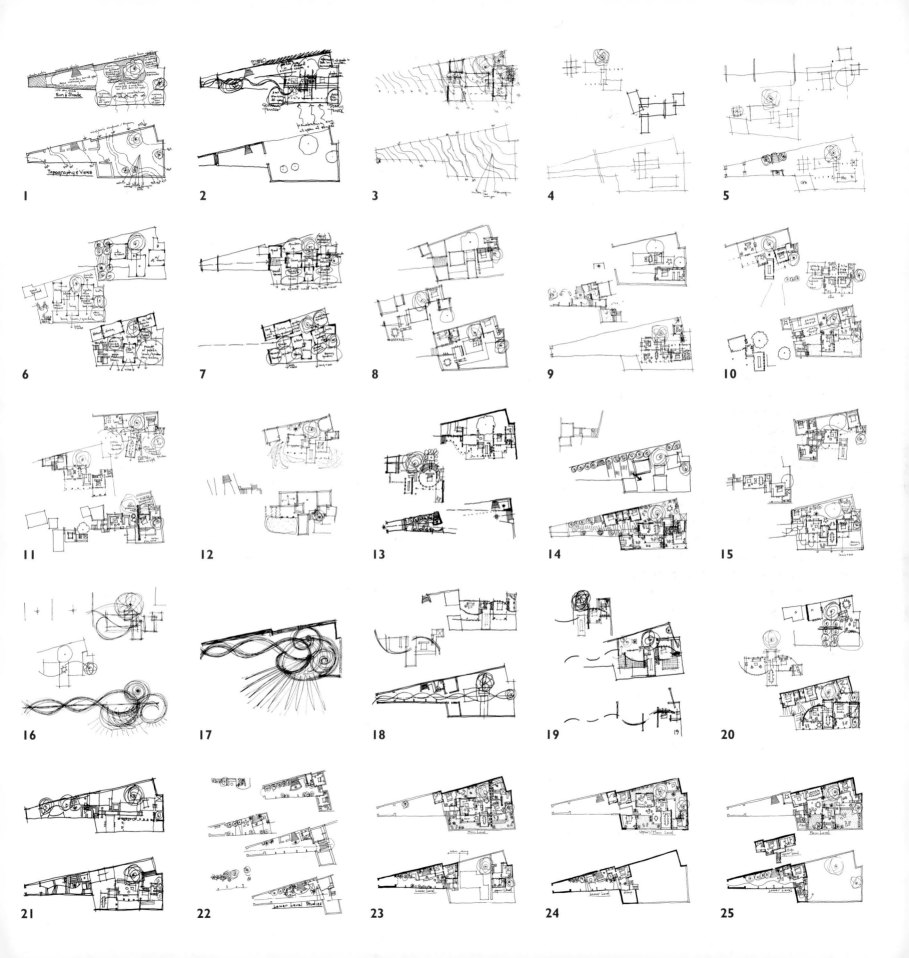

1

2

3

4

5

6

7

8

9

10

11

12

13

14

15

16

17

18

19

20

21

22

23

24

25

We try, through our process, to allow our clients to realize their dreams, to find the voice that may be suppressed, and to comfortably make decisions. Over the years we have developed a comprehensive questionnaire that serves many purposes. Some of the questions are straightforward: how big is your dining table, are there any special health considerations, who cooks, who cleans, when do you shower or bathe, what appliances do you use? Other questions deal with personal habits: are you quiet or outgoing, do you like the sun to wake you, are you casually or meticulously organized, what are your art preferences, hobbies, exercise, and spiritual practices? Then there are more probing personal questions: do you trust your intuition, after an argument how do you make up, what most frustrates you about the home you live in now, do you change your mind often, if so, why? And there are questions meant to elicit feelings from another part of their minds: describe a place you were very happy as a child, describe a smell you love, how would you like this home to make you feel when you come home after a difficult day, name the special places you have traveled, what is your most important piece of furniture? There are specific questions about the use of each room, about materials, storage, gardens, and so on. Of course it helps us understand the client, but, even more importantly, it helps them think about things that will serve in developing the design of their home. Our clients often learn something new about each other and these questions stimulate everyone involved into a more meaningful, complex dialogue. What we learn can be startling, revealing, and intimate, but always useful and insightful revelations into our clients' innermost feelings and desires. Ultimately, it gives us all clear direction.

As the design is further developed and the project moves through stages of refinement, there are always choices that clarify how life might be lived that move the project closer to what it will become and bring in the possibility of poetic interpretation. Diagrammatic analysis shifts from the whole to the parts. Drawings become more detailed; models, either physical or virtual, are developed. During our first visit to a site and throughout the design process, we collect natural materials from the land—bark, leaves, rocks, soil, grasses, lichen, moss, and flowers—whatever defines the colors and textures of the site. In the end, these will help us find the colors and materials for the project—whether it will stand apart, in contrast to, or blend with the natural colors of the land—these materials guide us. They are spilled out onto our conference table and immediately other materials from our library start coming into play—the slate that perfectly blends with shades of bark, the plaster the color of the leaves in summer, the color that draws the subtleties out of a stem in the grasses and glows in the afternoon sun … In our office workshop we mix plasters and stains, paints and dyes, selecting materials for floors and cabinets, counters and walls. Our extensive reference library becomes useful to our clients as photographs are tagged and sent home with stacks of books to help clarify image and communication. Discussions of budget are frequent for a clear understanding in the consequences of each choice. Every material and piece of equipment, every color, special treatment, and process for construction will ultimately be selected and defined. It is always our hope that there is no looking back or regret in the direction and decisions.

Design Development

To illustrate the further development of design we have chosen a variety of visual techniques from a number of different projects, at various stages of progress. All of these are actual projects, some built and included in this book, others unbuilt or in progress at this time.

26 Sections cut through different areas of a new home in Mexico showing relationships of interior and courtyard spaces. **27** Elevation studies for the street façade showing possible compositions for the front door, windows and terrace above for Casa Estrellas. **28** Perspective view of master bedroom and terrace and surrounding garden areas for Palo Colorado. **29** Sections cut through the building showing interior elevations and relationships between interior and exterior spaces for a new home in Mexico. **30** Sketch showing tile mural design and color layout in the shower/bathtub of Calle Paloma. **31** Initial elevation studies for wall, window and roof configurations for Casa de Buenas Almas. **32** Perspective study of possible master bathroom layout for a new home in the Caribbean. **33** Twelve alternative layouts for the children's bathroom in Dos Iguanas. **34** Interior perspective showing a stairway with wooden grid railing and display niche for a new home in St. Augustine, Florida. **35** Interior elevation studies for first floor areas in a new home in Mexico. **36** Section cut through Casa Joya showing vertical relationships of spaces with furniture and art on the walls. **37** Design studies for the tile mural on the master bathroom wall in Casa Estrellas. **38** Ground floor plan with gardens for a new home in St. Augustine, Florida. **39** Design studies for the steps from the dining terrace to the pool in Dos Iguanas. **40** Exterior perspective and color study for a new home in California. **41** Ground floor plan of a home with multiple courtyards and an interior salt water swimming pool on a Caribbean Island. **42** Cut-away isometric view of Casa Estrellas. **43** Steel railing designs for a new home on the Sea of Cortes. **44** Upper floor plan of a new home on the Sea of Cortes in Mexico with terraces and ramp with layered planters. **45** Alternative plan studies for Casa Estrellas. **46** Interior view of a new home in San Francisco. **47** Construction details for windows in Sleepy Hollow. **48** Section cut through the stairway in Dos Iguanas showing sculpting of stair, window, and cabinet at landing, balcony, and niche under stair for a plant. **49** Plans for new home in Mexico with three courtyards showing furniture and gardens. **50** Exterior perspective study for home in St. Augustine, Florida.

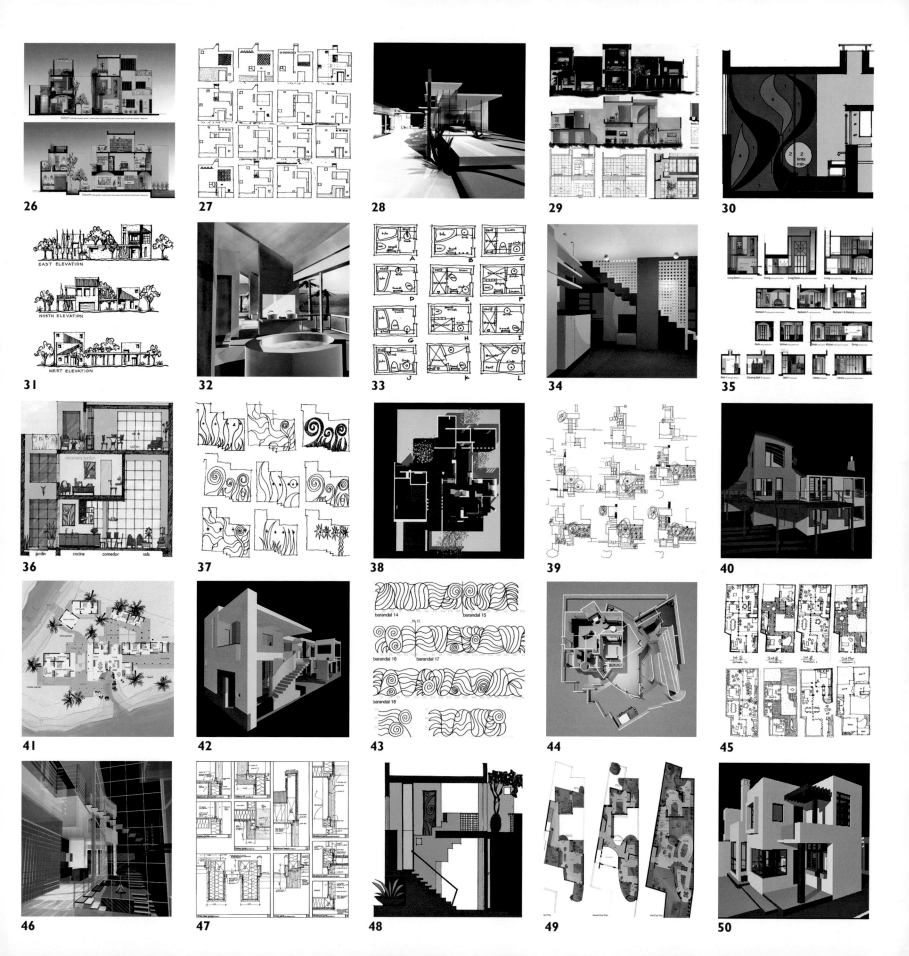

26

27

28

29

30

31

32

33

34

35

36

37

38

39

40

41

42

43

44

45

46

47

48

49

50

The texture of the land changes hour by hour in the wine country of Northern California. Shadows, long and sharp, sweep over rugged outcroppings and rolling hills; soft mist flows across the terrain below peaks that pierce through to crystalline blue skies and boundless views. A long country road meanders past orderly rows of grape stakes to chaotic shafts of light blinking through firs and redwoods, ending at a west-facing ridge. Stark land, rugged boulders, gnarled bark on multi-trunk oaks and two lizards sunning themselves said 'this is home' to a San Francisco couple looking for a place to redefine themselves and start a family. An artist hidden within a venture capitalist, a mother hidden within a business executive, both needed room to develop and touch the land in a way not possible in the City. With a boulder as anchor point and sun paths for layout, this home is rooted in the site as though it has grown there naturally. Emerging from the trees into the clearing, the view is only glimpsed before stepped building blocks invite entry into the courtyard. Barren earth pierced with boulders and sliced by sheets of steel leads to the soaring, light-filled entry gallery. Linking public and private spaces, this volume is streaked with light from tall windows and carefully placed skylights, each revealing form and color in

DOS IGUANAS

the geometries of material. Solid forms of red and ochre stucco cast strong shadows and lay against each other in constantly changing compositions, contrasting the intense blue sky and deep green pines. Massive cedar timbers in trellises and window frames echo the charcoal-gray weathered bark of oak clusters. The living room offers broad windows to the vista, as well as strong, solid walls, shaped to contain fire and art; the dining room's large windows frame focused views. The kitchen gazes to the side yard, with its dining nook and terrace inviting introspective focus on food and conversation. A cascading stairway descends to the pool terrace, the full breadth of the view revealed as water soars into space and the hillside drops off. Bedrooms and studies at the second floor are linked with an open, skylit sitting area overlooking the entry below. Splayed windows and slits of skylights track the sun through the seasons. Recycled wood flooring glows warm, a peaceful foundation for walls that are sculpted into niches and seats, ledges and closets. Planes of color focus movement from space to space, creating a journey of discovery as form, light, and surprising vistas unfold. In this world of gentle climate, terraces on every side of this home link living to nature in a seamless embrace.

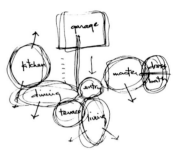

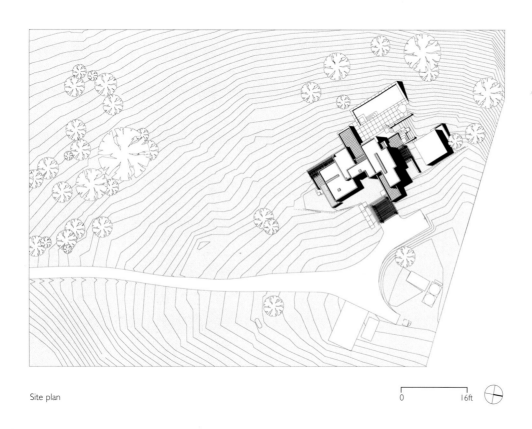

Site plan

0   16ft

The compositions of forms align, move, and transform as they are encountered, from solid to light, from light into shadow, from welcome to embrace.

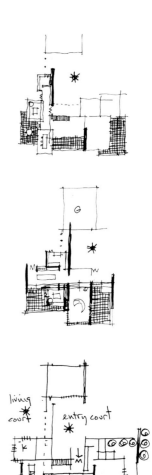

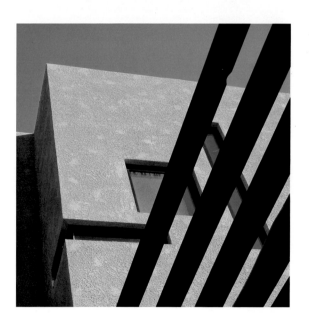

Composition, proportion, movement, focus, vista, color, texture, light, reflection, pause, glimpse, surprise, wonder, and joy are our tools in shaping space. We take great pleasure in discovering how to use them in unique ways for each client to create homes that embrace and celebrate their lives.

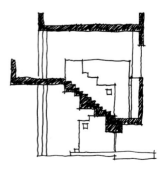

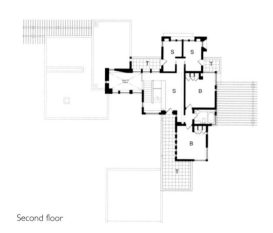

Second floor

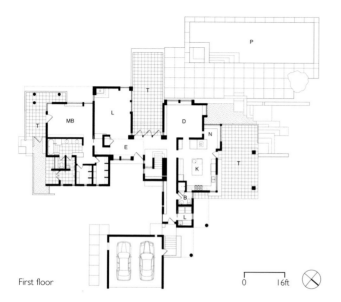

First floor

0   16ft

"Form comes from wonder. Wonder stems from our in-touchness with how we were made. The first feeling must have been a sense of beauty." – Louis Kahn

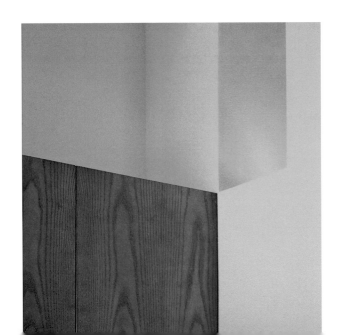

Color, texture, and light are inextricably intertwined and can have a profound effect on our emotions. Sometimes they define individual spaces or celebrate materials. They may focus attention, define one form against another, separate foreground from background or create a unifying link between spaces.

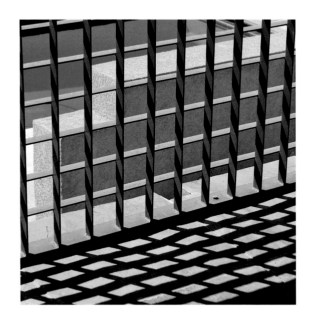

In a quiet Mexican neighborhood where sounds of children playing and stark shadows of brilliant sunlight delineate a rich culture, this small home above a garage and studio is phase one of a larger dream. With natural light flooding in on three sides, the sun's movement overlays interior spaces that respond to the owner's lifestyle. Bi-folding glass doors open the living areas to morning light, shafts of sun from three skylights washing the walls throughout the day. Spaces are subtly articulated by cabinets and wall fragments. The large window in the living room extrudes from the face of the building to provide a long, built-in desk area. The bedroom is open, yet private, with deep bookcases serving both bedroom and living room, with niches for art and a television that pivots around to serve both rooms. A three-sided fireplace floats above the polished concrete floor, its flames dancing among layers of broken black glass, a perforated, hand-hammered copper screen above reflecting sparkles of light and fire onto the walls. Sunsets over distant mountains illuminate an intimate terrace off the bedroom. A wall of frosted glass between the kitchen and bathroom bathes the shower in soft morning light. Polished charcoal-gray concrete counters with integrally formed sinks are imbued with a tactile complexity from hand troweling, a texture that continues on to the multi-tonal concrete floor. Cabinets of vertical grain mahogany

CALLE PALOMA

stained in deep-red, ebony, and forest green complement the broken tile mural wrapping the shower, folding into niches and windows. The first-floor studio is designed for glass-making and gallery space with room for a car. A sculpted stairway climbs to the living terrace with fluttering ribbons of steel railings and intertwining shadows decorating the walls in shifting patterns. The stair to the roof is inspired by one we discovered by chance in a tiny Greek chapel. Steel doors and windows handcrafted by the blacksmith are hand-perforated and naturally rusted at the entry and garage doors. Phase two includes a two-story steel-and-glass living space with an office floating above the kitchen. Herb and flower gardens in homage to the owner's grandmother will fill exterior spaces, with sculpted steps to a private master suite. Sustainability has been a guiding force in this home of concrete and brick, constructed entirely by hand, without power tools, by local craftsmen with local materials. Though the fireplace can heat the entire space, the thermal mass of the sun-warmed concrete floor radiates warmth long after sunset. Trellises and window shades control the summer sun, windows and skylights provide natural ventilation, the gas water heater is on-demand, lights are LED, and the roof is planted green. Rainwater collected in an underground cistern is used for irrigation and purified for drinking. Future gardens will supply organic herbs and produce, wrap the home in fragrance, and ensure daily communion with the land.

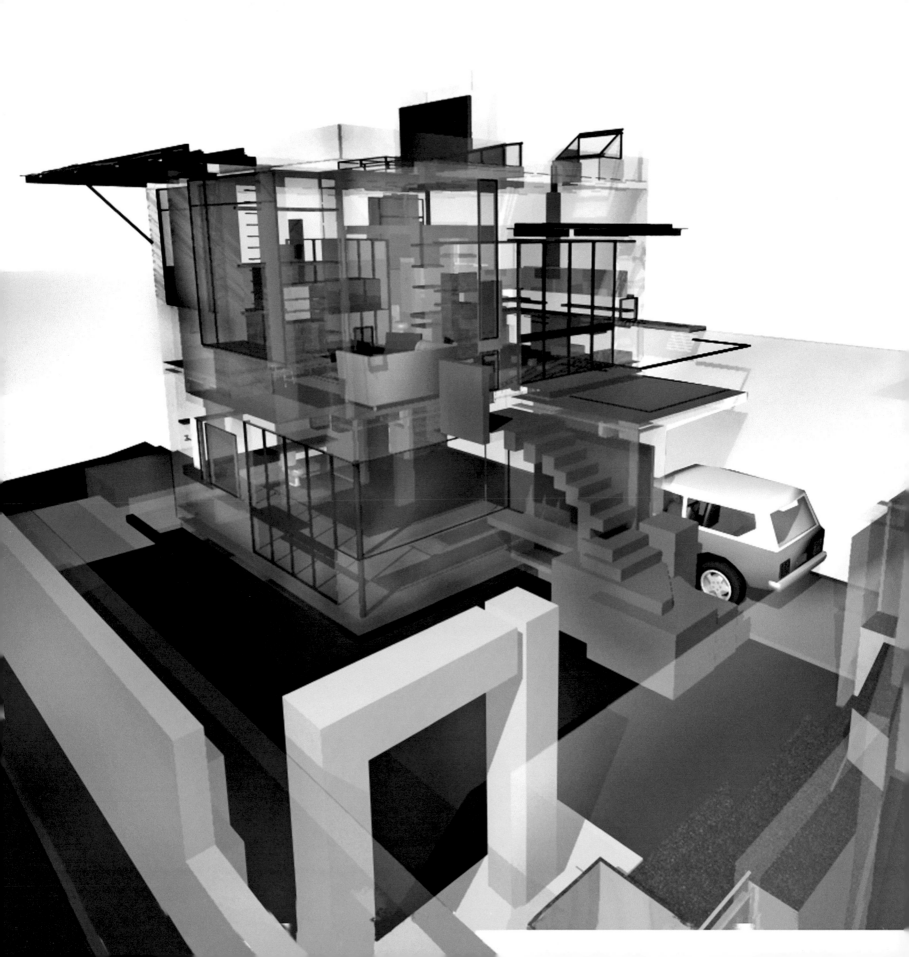

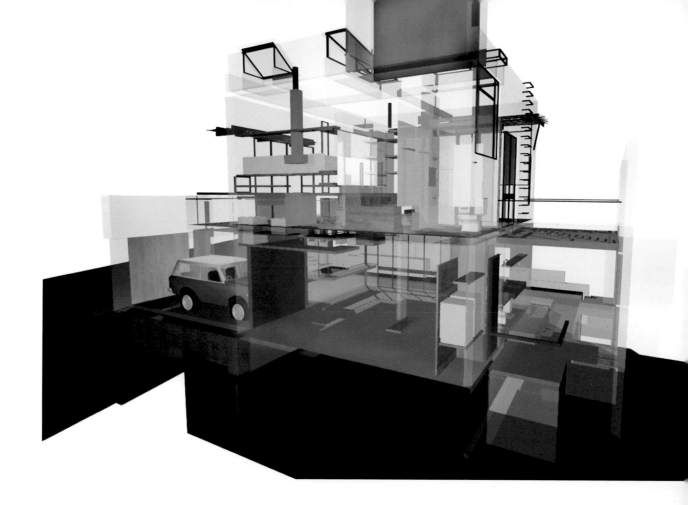

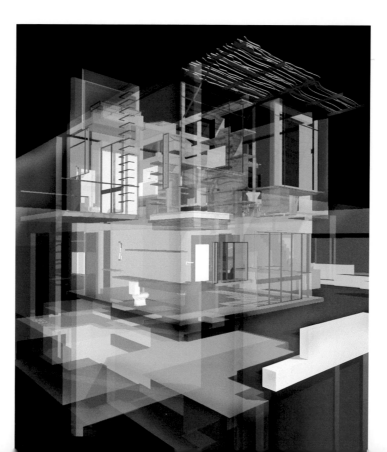

Three-dimensional railings flutter in a constant dance with their shadows. Set against the stark, simple forms of the building, these moving elements have a life of their own, full of surprise and delight.

Light is a living presence, intimately tactile as it washes across textured and mottled surfaces. The floor plan is simple but the spaces unfold in unexpected complexity.

First floor

Second floor

0   18ft

The monochromatic body of the building is imbued with tonal variations of reflected color from interior elements, as well as shifts in hue from light washes at different times of day. This modulation of color and light is magnified in the multi-tonal qualities of the handmade tiles, the polished concrete, and the hammered copper.

The idea of enveloping a piece of the outdoors into the center of a home has developed in almost every culture where man has dreamed of perfect spatial balance. Even in ancient Egypt, homes excavated near the Valley of the Kings were discovered to have an interior garden. North of San Francisco in the Anderson Valley, on a former horse ranch covered with wild California grasses and mature oaks, pines, and Douglas-fir trees, this 60-foot-by-60-foot square home with an interior garden courtyard manifests a simple, Zen-like form within an untamed landscape. Built for an industrial designer and an artist, this retreat is completely wrapped with corrugated galvanized steel, reflecting the sky and trees, changing color throughout the day, sometimes sparkling and at other times almost invisible. The guiding force behind the home's design was our clients' dream to create a sanctuary, a serene place for creative work, reflection, and cooking, with open spaces, abundant indirect natural light, and a strong connection to the outdoors. By wrapping the rooms around an interior courtyard, fresh air and natural light permeate into the very heart of this home, allowing every space to enjoy light and views on two sides. Rooms, unencumbered by traditional divisions, flow

ANDERSON VALLEY

together, each unfolding around the corner from the next, open yet separated by cabinetry, floating display walls, or a two-sided fireplace. Deep-set porches on the south and west sides offer shade from the strong summer sun and provide covered outdoor space in which to sit quietly. The reversed roof slope at the studio opens a tall wall of glass to filtered morning light, closing down to all other direct sun. Broad expanses of composed windows puncture walls to frame selected views to the hills and canyons beyond, as well as to the central garden courtyard where a Japanese maple and a rock fountain provide a tranquil meditation area. An 8-foot square glass entry door with a red steel frame delineates a transparent focal point in the approach to the home. Simplicity and functionality were vital considerations in the selection of finish materials and the color palette. Corrugated galvanized steel siding and roofing are anchored with a red concrete column supporting the roof overhang. Black slate floors, bleached maple cabinetry with zinc and stone counters, contemporary light fixtures and brilliant white walls provide a clean, modern backdrop for the owners' eclectic collection of paintings, furniture, ceramics, and ethnic art.

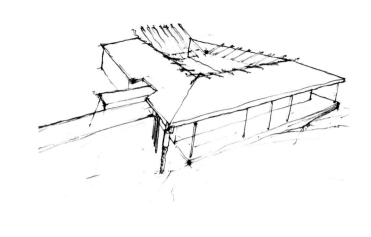

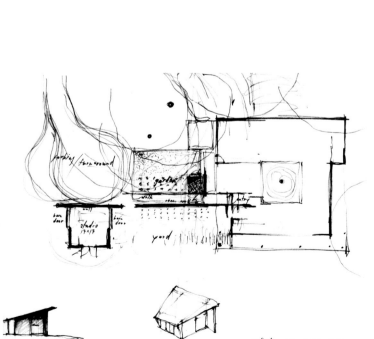

palladian villa in the hill

Site plan

0   32ft

The relatively small dimension of the central courtyard, surrounded on three sides by tall walls, allows for large windows without the need for shades or coverings. The sun is never in position long enough to feel intrusive before an adjacent wall or roof angle changes the intensity. Small clerestory windows invite rays of sunlight to create surprise unexpectedly or wash luminous reflections across alabaster walls.

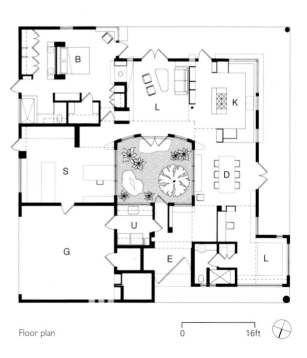

Floor plan

0   16ft

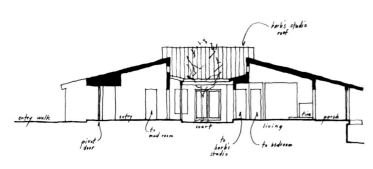

Nelson Residence, section (cut east to west)
scale - 1/8" : 1'-0"

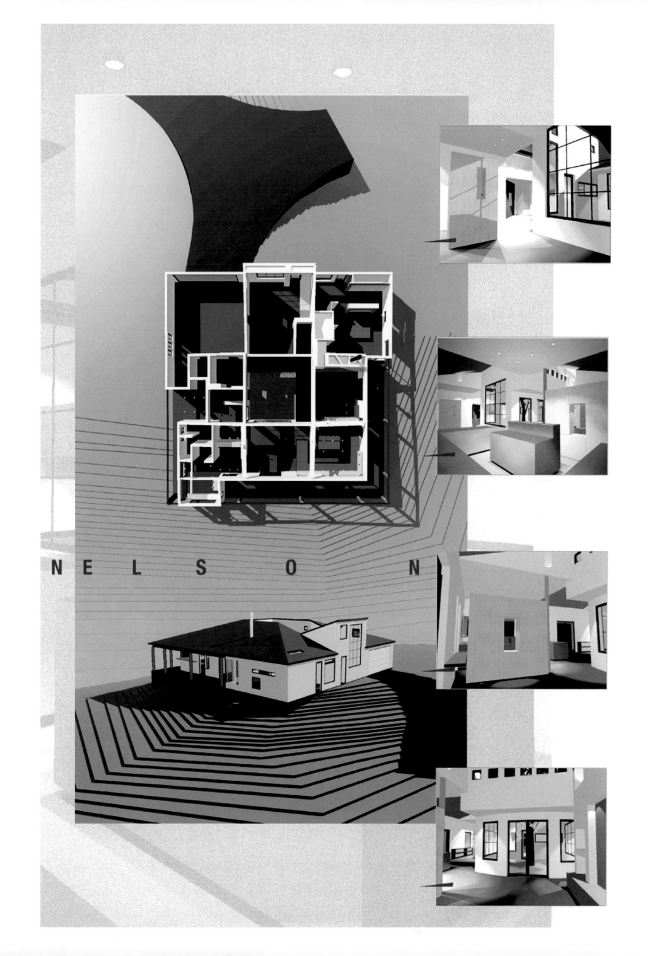

NELSON

The master bed floats above the slate floor, a tranquil island embraced by its wide surround, evoking a feeling of separation yet deliberately anchored to the free-standing headboard with a deep niche. The large square window is set for perfect viewing from laying down, while the long horizontal window provides a slender slice of view from the master vanity sinks behind the headboard.

We discovered the beautiful old colonial town of San Miguel de Allende by chance in 1989 while searching for a quarry for Mexican cantera stone. We fell in love with Mexico and with its people, bought a little ruin in the historic center and built a home, a retreat where we nourish our creative souls. The sounds of the crickets echo against the walls of our courtyard, the last rays of sunlight fade into a luminescent glow, music from a fiesta nearby calls us to explore what is going on—but the embrace of our walls is too inviting and we want only to stay and dream. In this land of possibility, there is something that makes us feel the extraordinary in the every day, which opens our awareness to powerful subtleties. San Miguel is Mexico at its best, frozen in time yet alive in every way. Indians dance holy rituals across from contemporary art galleries in ancient courtyards. Church bells peal out the hours and deep colors fading on ancient walls glow under crystalline skies. Bougainvillea cascades, aromas waft, music and laughter fill the air. Seven years after we built our home we had the opportunity to buy a second little ruin and build another home. This tiny property had much to say about how a home could fit and flow. Some aspects of the design of this

CASA ESTRELLAS

"house of stars" stem from historical influences, some from the indigenous evolution of ideas, a way of living or building that evolves directly from the land, and some are from our dreams. This is a dense urban setting where homes touch each other, holding wide to their property lines, opening to a central courtyard. That is a beautiful tradition, which we fully embrace. Circulation through the courtyard not only allows each of the rooms to flow into the garden, but air and light pour into every space. Rooms with large windows are open, yet completely private. Luscious mango, cobalt, and sage colors are made from natural pigments washed on to layer forms against each other, creating compositions to pull the eye and define the spaces. Red and ochre river rocks are hand-set against a charcoal stone background in the courtyard paving. Materials are local, as are the construction techniques, but the forms are a product of organic geometries that align life in this home to the sun, the wind, and views to the many church towers. We are contemporary California architects working in a world that is changing quickly, working to create homes that are completely contemporary and absolutely traditional as well. This home is strong, transparent, layered in color, form, and emotion. It is modern, but saturated with the deepest of Mexican tradition.

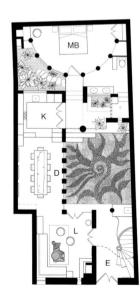

First floor

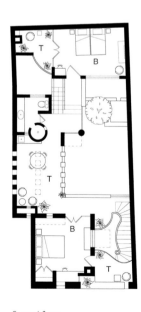

Second floor

0   16ft

Grids of steel windows span from floor to ceiling, opening each room to gardens and light, linking inside to outside in an invisible embrace. A row of square columns between the dining room and courtyard invites shafts of light to spill inside. A 200-year-old carpenter's table is suspended in a new wood frame to become the 11-foot-long dining table, surrounded by antique woven leather seat chairs from America's old West.

The master bedroom sits slightly above the courtyard, a deep-blue wall against which an arc of burnished columns stand, opening the room to a private garden. A colorful tile mural and a glass-beaded seat in the shower of the master bathroom are sprinkled with droplets of sun filtered through an ancient pomegranate tree.

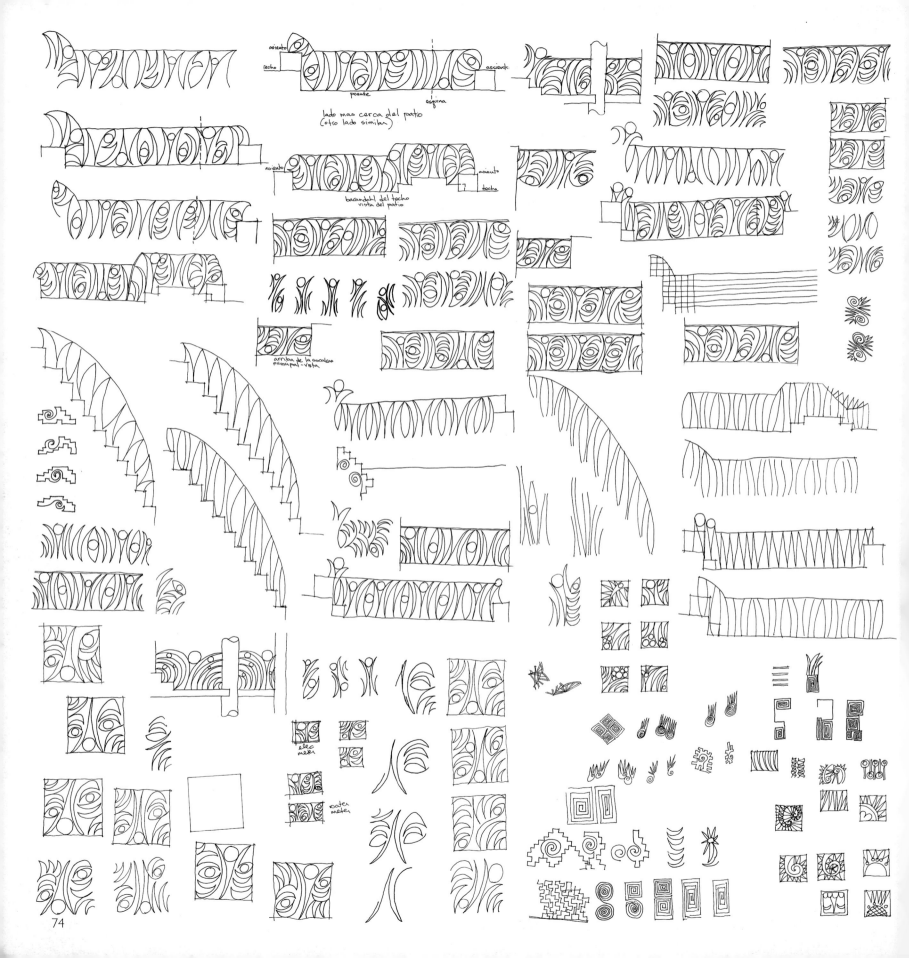

lado mas cerca del patio
(otro lado similar)

asiento
techo
puente
esquina
asiento

asiento
asiento
techo

barandal del techo
vista del patio

arriba de la escalera
principal - vista

elec
metr

water
meter

74

The deep-blue courtyard wall, sprinkled with frosted-glass star lights, flows into the entry, a calm background to the sinuous stairway and whimsical steel railings. Bedrooms at the second floor, each with a private balcony, share a covered terrace and a glass-topped cylindrical shower.

"Architecture is not only buildings but all that man makes with his hands in the course of his daily occupations." – Martin Heidegger

On a small city lot in San Francisco's Marina district, a poorly maintained 100-year-old duplex stood waiting for the right family to rescue it from decay. Over the years a series of sheds had been added on to the rear of the original gabled box to create a disparate array of jumbled forms. A young couple planning to begin their family found in the building the seeds of a contemporary single-family home. This building is located on a narrow, dead-end street, so access was a challenge, as were the restrictive zoning regulations for this neighborhood of older, smaller-scale, turn-of-the-century dwellings. Removal of the rear sheds uncovered the building's original form and opened space for a more thoughtful addition. The original building was particularly well placed and scaled for its lot, set back from the street, with a 6-foot-wide side yard and a rear garden. There was room within the allowable building envelope for a 17-foot by 21-foot addition, within which a two-story living space and a master suite were planned. The original building was gutted to make room for a garage, a powder room, and a long, slender dining room at the lower floor, and children's bedrooms, bathroom, and

H A R R I S   P L A C E

a loft–family area at the second floor. From the street, the house maintains its original scale in line with its neighbors. Rich ochre-colored stucco over the old siding, a new concrete and slatted wood garden wall, and a wood garage door are respectful of the setting, adding serenity to the street. Entry is through an intimate garden at the front, continuing through a lush side garden to the centrally located front door beneath a galvanized steel awning. The living room spills onto a sunny wood deck and the garden at the rear where mature vegetation provides privacy for a new hot tub. Though tightly surrounded by adjacent dwellings, this home is a garden oasis, full of light and views. High ceilings, carefully placed windows, and skylights create light-filled, sculpted spaces, detailed with bamboo flooring, steel cable railings, and a zinc fireplace surround. Old industrial light fixtures and hardware are mixed with new throughout. Maple cabinetry, hand-packed concrete counters, stainless steel appliances, antique tables, classic furniture, and an eclectic collection of art represent the owners' tastes, comfortable in this new "City" home.

The dining room opens into the side garden with two pairs of French doors. The kitchen connects directly to the living and dining spaces with long views through the side garden. In the loft–family area overlooking the living room, former attic space recaptured from the original gabled roof becomes a secret children's escape.

The master suite at the third floor, reached by a choreographed journey that gives it separation, is a private retreat where a softly vaulted ceiling frames views to the Golden Gate and the surrounding neighborhood. Skylights and large, deeply set windows provide natural light at every turn.

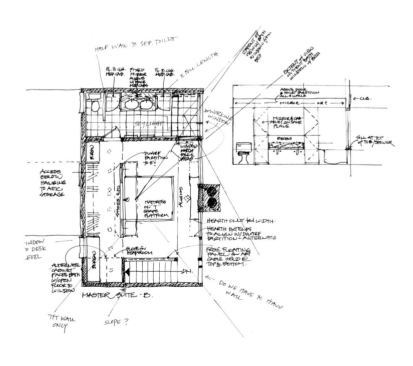

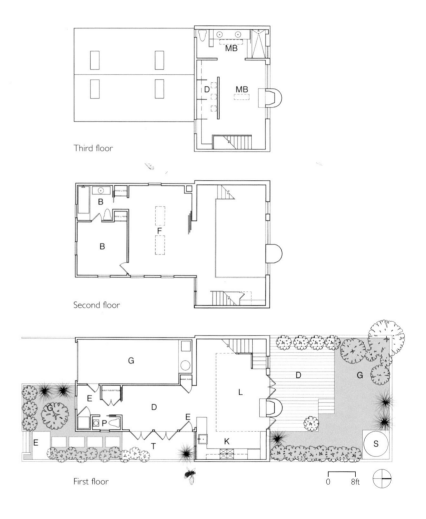

Third floor

Second floor

First floor

0   8ft

Holidays spent in the Sierra Mountains, along the Pacific coast and in the desert eventually led our clients to Baja, Mexico. On a journey to view the 1991 solar eclipse, they discovered the remote fishing village of Cabo Pulmo on the Sea of Cortes. This harsh, lonely landscape of thorny brush and magnificent mountains touched our clients' hearts and they knew it would become part of their lives. 'Casa de Buenas Almas' (Home of the Good Souls), is a compound of three small buildings wrapped around an old tree whose gnarled branches have been sculpted by the elements. Each component of the triad—house, guesthouse, and garage—responds to views, breezes, vegetation, and days that include reading, music, cooking, bird-watching, walking on the beach, and sharing meaningful time with friends, family, and their dogs Lieba and Pica. Old Mexican urns flank the main entry and five sets of antique hacienda doors integrated into the portals of each space as hurricane shutters are visual reminders of the history of this land. Living, dining, and kitchen flow together under a high ceiling, open in each direction to a view, a breeze, an outdoor space, or an element of the landscape. Palapa-covered terraces provide outdoor cooking and dining, with wide, built-in benches for visiting, napping, and watching clouds. The master bedroom, bath, study, balcony, and terrace are

CASA DE BUENAS ALMAS

reached by an open stairway, an intimate retreat overlooking the mountains, sea, and rugged landscape, nurturing the profound connection our clients feel to this land. A separate 'casita' is a private home for guests with its own rhythms, harmonious as a sculptural element in the vistas from every side of the compound. Each window, each place to stand, sit, or pass through, is carefully composed to create powerful connections between nature and the rituals of life. Glass blocks puncture walls in seemingly random patterns, providing sparkles of light at different times of day, or, along with a floating concrete shelf, turn the back of the garage into the third face of the triad embracing the central courtyard. Large gridded windows and multiple terraces capture tropical breezes and frame views to the mountains, the sea, and the other elements of this home. Careful orientation offers protection from the hot Tropic of Cancer sun and the cold winter winds. Colors derive from the soft purple haze of the mountains and their bold salmon-colored outcroppings. The stained concrete floors, countertops, sink, and tub are spare and mottled by hand construction, soft and tactile in their finish. In this remote location devoid of power and phone lines, electricity is gathered from the sun to supply all the comforts of home.

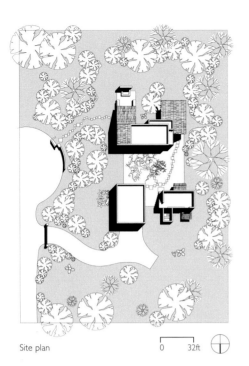

Site plan

0   32ft

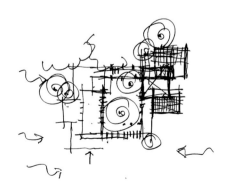
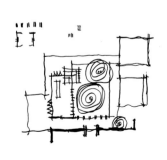
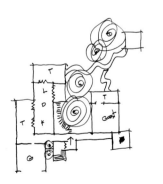
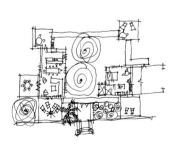

Rhythms come in many forms. They can be as regular as a row of columns, as irregular as scattered small windows, as orderly as steps, even organic as in the leaves, shadows, and passing moments. Rhythms are all around us; they give order to our world. They give us calm, serenity, and surprise. The rhythms of our heartbeats, our breath, are modulated by those other rhythms we encounter as we move through life.

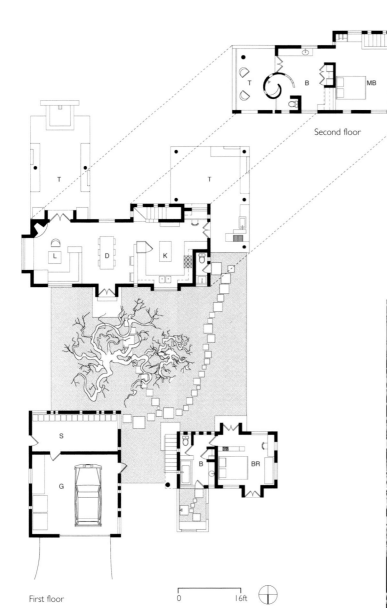

Second floor

First floor

0 ——————— 16ft

Embrace can be felt in the brush of a shadow, the reflection of a color, the branches of a tree. The warmth of the sun, the view to a mountain, the passing of a cloud, even these can embrace us. Architecture that embraces does not have to contain, for embrace is made real by that feeling of peaceful boundaries, thoughtfully, soulfully constructed around us.

1.

2.

3.

4.

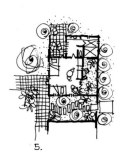
5.

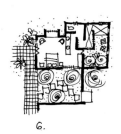
6.

Some journeys home are long and circuitous. Leaving the Soviet Union while the Iron Curtain still divided the world, in search of a new life, our clients made their way to the San Francisco Bay Area. Unable to find a contemporary home they wanted to live in, they came to us after seeing one we had designed for another client. Though both engineers, they had hearts of poets when it came to working together on the design of their home. Their sense of dimension and attention to even the tiniest detail permeated every thought and made them excellent collaborators. Private in many ways, they enjoy sharing their home to celebrate special moments in the lives of their friends, often with large gatherings. In a suburban neighborhood of traditional houses close to the street with garage doors dominating their façades, this new home is set deep into its lot with its garage turned at 90 degrees to the street to provide both privacy and a carefully choreographed arrival. This distance prolongs the journey home and offers a serene final approach along a curving drive through a gracious front garden. The disconnection from neighboring houses envelops this home in an aura of safety and seclusion. Strong geometric forms are linked and interlocked with thick walls and

BUTTERNUT

broad bands of gridded windows, softened by gently vaulted roofs and an elegant palette of colors and materials. Wide slate steps lead to a massive mahogany entry door set within a deep, thick frame, bisecting the main gallery and continuing through to a swath of luminous green grass. Standing-seam roofing in a metallic champagne color complements the muted shades and textures of taupe stucco. A 26-foot-high skylit gallery links public and private activities and floods this home with natural light. The long central gallery ends in framed views to clusters of flaming amber trees. Casual activities center in the large family room, open to rear terraces and the grassy yard. For formal gatherings, the dining room takes a more solitary, internal position, accessible yet set apart, with broad views toward both the front and rear gardens. The living room and library are separated from the activities of daily life to provide a quiet retreat. A secondary gallery links the garage and rear entry directly with the kitchen and family room. A sculpted stairway leads to the bedrooms and children's play area with a bridge flying through the double-height, sky-lit spaces to the master suite. High vaulted ceilings embrace each sleeping area, clerestory windows adding sparkling light throughout the day.

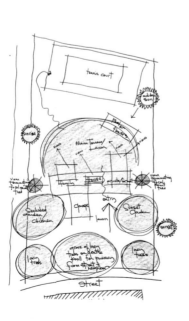

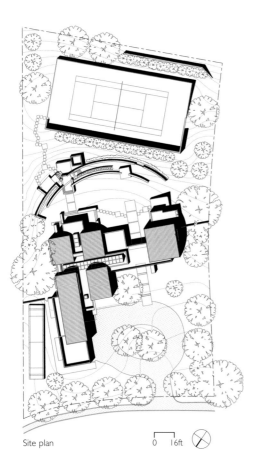

Site plan

0   16ft

Concrete pavers link outdoor terraces and sculpted steps twist and overlap past curving layered cutting gardens to a spa and tennis court below.

The gardens appear greener when seen against the contrasting burnt-orange and mahogany walls. Densely planted, the narrow side gardens at the ends of the gallery allow large windows to comfortably face neighboring homes without window coverings.

The living room and library are wrapped in thick, sculpted walls with a zigzag sweep of glass modulated with mahogany pillars opening to the rear garden and distant views. Soft shades of taupe are accented with burnt-orange walls, red marble, black and green granite, and a deep-chocolate Brazilian stone figured like marbled paper.

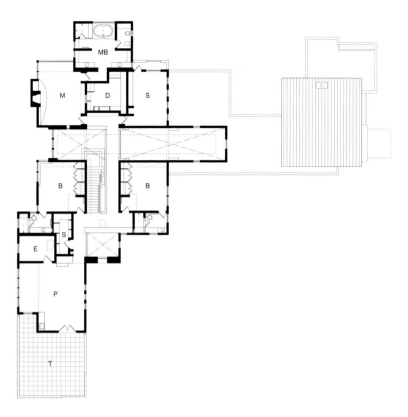

Second floor

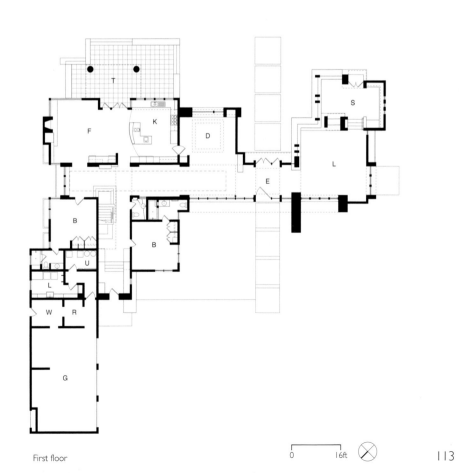

First floor

0   16ft

Rich tropical mahogany, shimmering golden anigre, and ebony woods lace together into cabinetry, railings and floating shelves. Fluttering sheets of paper glow as the light fixture above the dining table.

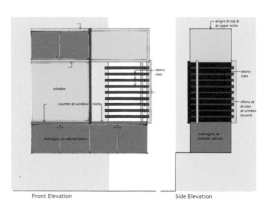

Front Elevation   Side Elevation

Cabinets are made from golden anigre wood, book-matched to produce a three-dimensional shimmer, and rich tropical mahogany. The kitchen counter granite has muted green crystal formations that give the appearance of gazing into the depths of the sea, complementing the soft limestone and red birch flooring. Reflected in a wall of mirror, soft light through cloud-like undulations in a sheet of polished alabaster infuse the room with a tactile glow.

The stairway is a folded ribbon of rich tropical mahogany flanked with slabs of shimmering anigre. Each move must be appropriate and thoughtful. Materials should touch each other with respect and joy. Movement should be a dance, not just for the body, but for the eyes and for the spirit.

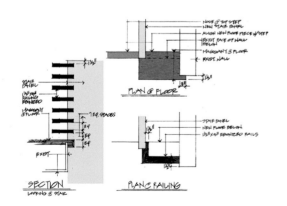

A classic 1950s ranch house overlooking San Francisco Bay served its owners, but as their family and needs grew, so did a desire for this home to more thoughtfully reflect their contemporary taste and lifestyle. Flat roofs with deep overhangs left interior spaces dark. Filled with outdated fixtures and appliances and awkward circulation, rooms were divided by walls and doors and connected by hallways. Poorly placed and almost never used, the front door was moved to the side of the house to create a processional link from the detached garage. A connecting breezeway roof was opened to pour light into a serene entry courtyard with a series of movable, red, slatted wood screens. Concrete stepping-stones lead across a mossy garden to a hand-troweled deep-mango-color plaster wall and African slate flooring at the new entry, making the experience of passing from the car to the house fluid and illuminated with surprise. A black slatted wood bench links inside and out at the new maple door. A new family room addition engages the living and dining rooms to become a large, open space comfortably divided into separate areas by sculpted elements—a crisp, hand-troweled plaster fireplace in the deep-mango color, maple walls gridded with aluminum channels, and changes in ceiling heights, materials and colors. A maple-

TEABERRY LANE

clad wall with floating shelves and a steel column mark points of departure and arrival. The kitchen was gutted, enlarged and re-planned with new stainless steel appliances, lighting, a combination of green laminate and maple cabinetry, and charcoal-gray tiles. Opening the wall between the kitchen and dining room with a large pass-through connects the spaces and captures views to the bay from the kitchen and to the hillside from the dining room. Black mosaic tile, a black toilet, and a long, custom stainless steel counter with integral sink add a new powder room where the original entry had been. Oak flooring was stained dark charcoal-gray and the existing ceiling was completely transformed by its new deep-red color. Exterior siding was stained the same rich dark charcoal-gray with the deep red on doors, railings, and exposed wood eaves. The rich and varied shades of black and gray in the bark and rugged cliff and the luscious red/oranges of the bird of paradise flowers were the elements of nature that inspired the new colors throughout, coordinating with the owner's contemporary furniture and art. Stainless steel cable railings at the new blackened wood deck invite a harmonious flow from inside to outside in this metamorphosis from bland to bold.

Passage from the detached garage to the new front door is a journey of discovery. Rather than making the path obvious, a series of sliding slatted walls and a simple garden with an opening in the breezeway roof for light and rain interrupt a straightforward connection and invite surprise. Translucent though solid, these screen walls heighten anticipation in this short, luminous path. The rhythms of the wood slats evoke a sense of serenity and movement becomes the portal into this home.

One of the joys in remodeling older homes is finding and preserving the soul in what exists and transforming the whole into a new entity. Small, isolated rooms with doors off hallways have opened to become luminous spaces that flow through each other, physically, visually, and spiritually. The intensity of the colors and contrasting textures bind this home to its site in spaces that nurture and celebrate an organic interconnectedness.

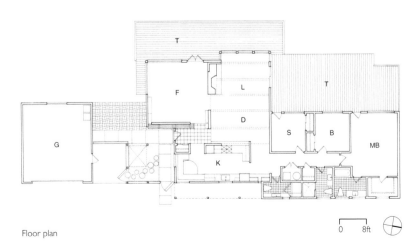

Floor plan

0   8ft

The simple, clean lines of maple and laminate cabinets, combined with stainless steel detailing and charcoal-gray mosaic tiles, all sitting on rich black flooring is a serene palette, allowing the elements of life—flowers, food, dishes—to be the art.

A wondrous life path that had meandered through Spain, France, New York, and California eventually wandered into a small town in the Central Highlands of Mexico. Having designed their home in San Francisco and developed a continuing friendship, we invited our friends and their two young children to enjoy our vacation home in San Miguel de Allende. It was love at first sight and they soon asked us to find them property and design a vacation home. What we found was a 10- by10-meter (33- by 33-foot) urban lot at the end of a narrow pedestrian lane in the historic center. Dimensions guided every design decision in order to fit a living room, dining room, kitchen, family room, three bedrooms, two bathrooms, powder room, as well as a courtyard, garden, terraces, and balconies onto this tiny piece of land. A 10-meter cube turned out to be the ideal size for a jewel box—*Una Casa de Joya*. Curving walls of glass and plaster link each space to the outdoors, swept with shimmers of sunlight that change throughout the day. A triangular spiral stairway spins movement up to the roof terrace, suspended above this fairy-tale village, for evening viewing of luminous sunsets—breathtakingly beautiful backdrops for myriad church towers and domes. Walls washed with naturally pigmented lime glow soft and warm under the sunlight

CASA JOYA

pouring through the skylight above the stairs. Spaces borrow from each other, layering together in the illusion of a grander volume. Twenty-foot-high ceilings in the living room with an 18-foot-high wall of gridded glass belie any sense that this is a small home. Bi-folding glass doors sweep walls away in the comfortable climate allowing inside and outside to flow together. A two-story stone fountain/water-wall sends ripples of light and sound throughout the home to complement the church bells, roosters, and calls from wandering vendors. Black cantera stone floors are locally quarried and the swirling stone pattern in the courtyard paving symbolizes the life path of the owners. Windows, doors, and whimsical railings are handmade by the blacksmith, the flaming sculpture in the fireplace assembled by the plumber, the gridded entry door, cabinets, and dining table that unfolds to seat ten fabricated by the carpenter in his open-air workshop. There is a sense of home, a sanctuary, in the airy glow of this liquid dream at the end of a long journey to this special place. The craftsmen who built this home have worked with us for more than 15 years, men who bring a spiritual joy to their work that stays behind in the places they build, imbuing them with an aura of magic.

We shape ourselves to fit this
world and by the world are
shaped again. The visible and
the invisible working together in
common cause, to produce the
miraculous. So may we, in this
life, trust to those elements we
have yet to see or imagine, and
look for the true shape of our
own self, by forming it well to the
great intangibles about us.

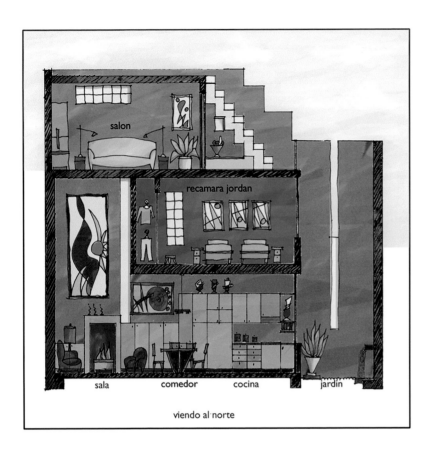

salon

recamara jordan

sala comedor cocina jardin

viendo al norte

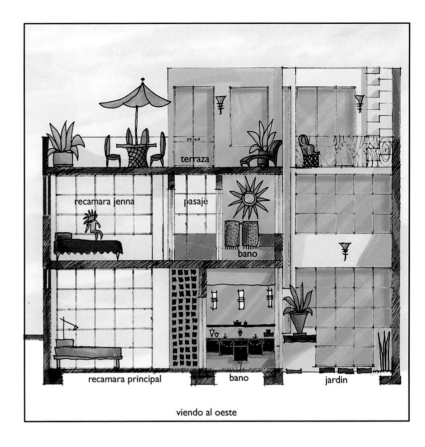

terraza

recamara jenna pasaje

bano

recamara principal bano jardin

viendo al oeste

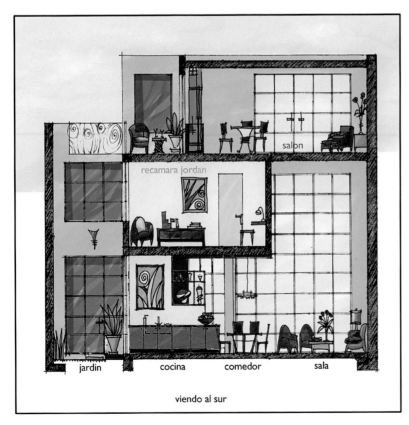

salon

recamara jordan

jardin cocina comedor sala

viendo al sur

patio sala

viendo al oeste

133

Third floor

Second floor

First floor

0   16ft

One of the pleasures in wandering secret lanes in Mexico is to discover what lies hidden behind the doors. Though touching neighboring homes, there is a sense of quiet seclusion, a private place at the end of a journey in this tiny, swirling, magic world. The embrace is tactile in the curving walls, the air heavy with color reflected on light that pours in throughout the day. Vistas are layered, views through grids of windows blend inside and out. Separation of spaces is subtle—a curve, a cabinet, a change in ceiling height, in color—yet there is a vastness felt in the way spaces flow together.

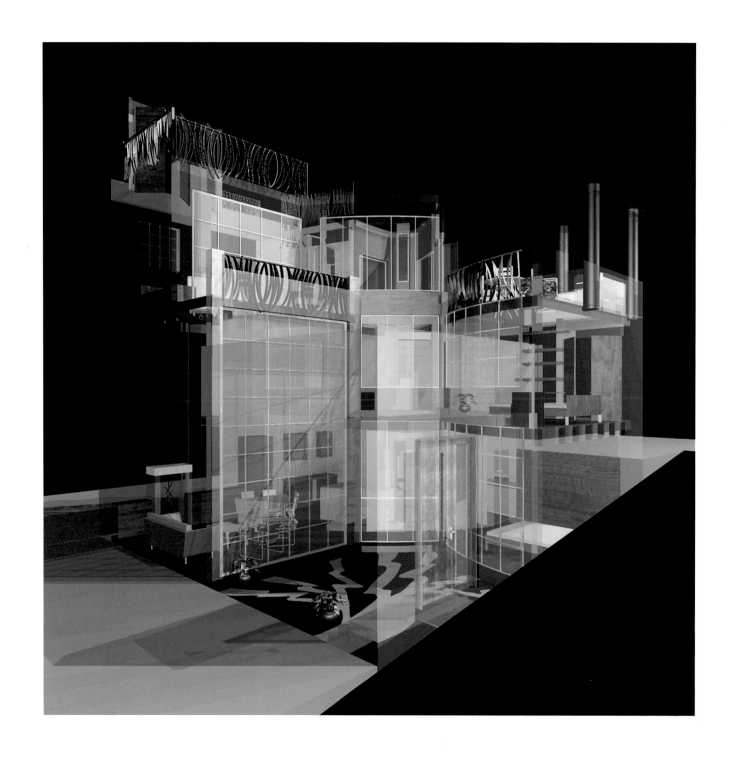

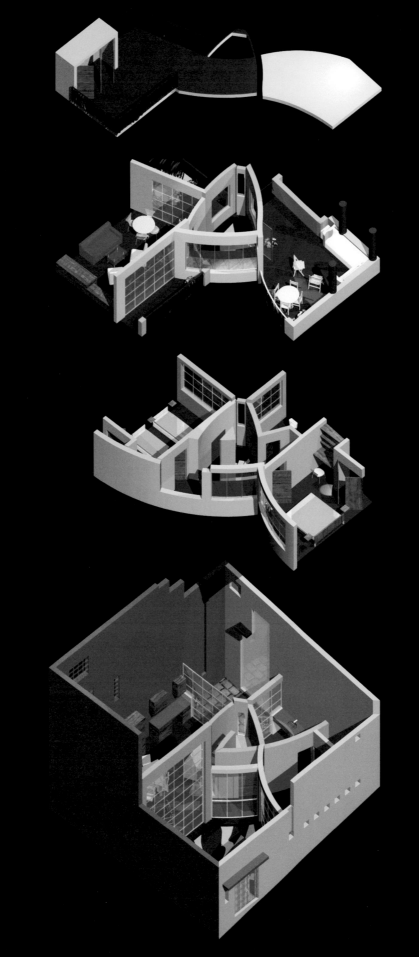

From the great architect Louis Kahn, there is a beautiful thought, which has always been an inspiration to us: "Material which was derived from light was spent light. Spent light was a material which cast a shadow by the grace of light, and the shadow belonged to the light. Silence met light. Light, the giver of all presence."

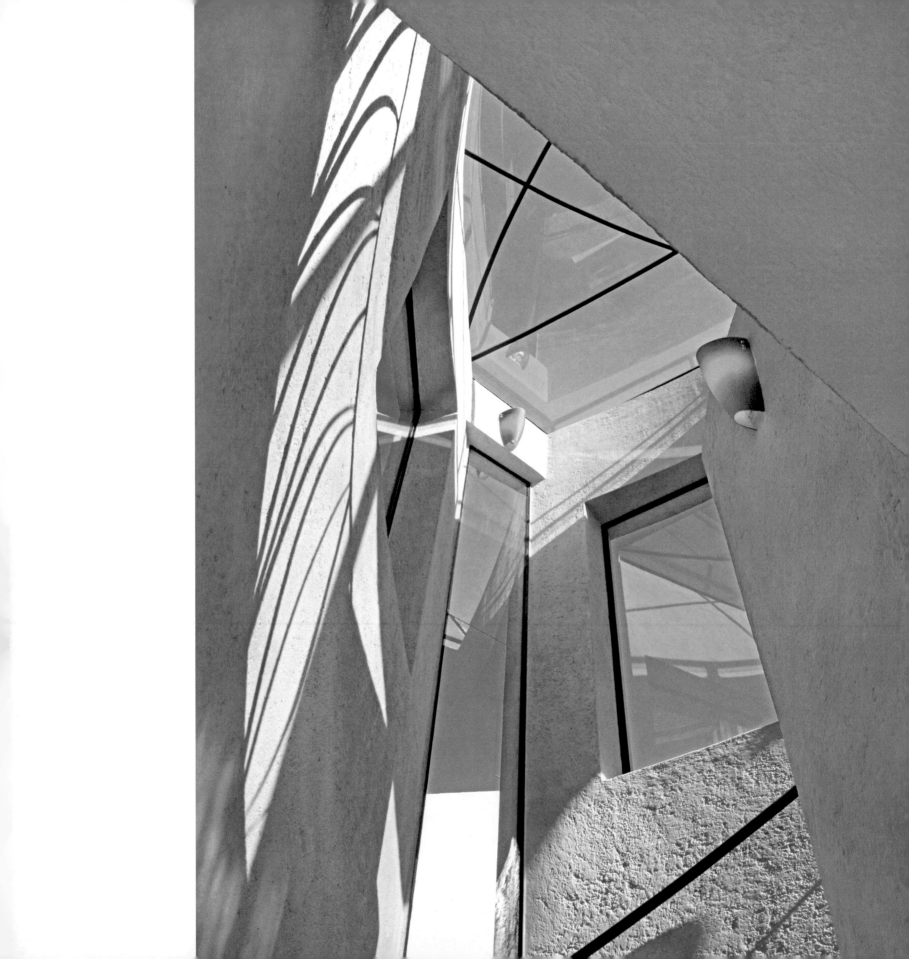

A steep triangular lot sliced by a deep, tree-lined ravine spoke to a young family with dreams of building a homestead, a modern 'ancestral' home. This was a journey of faith and discovery, a desire to establish roots and create a place with foundations broad enough to carry their vision of the future. A long driveway is the portal into their home—a calming culmination leading from freeways to city streets, up a country road, then from their entry gate, over a bridge and through the dense grove of bays and rugged oaks at the ravine. The garage is separated from the house, extending the journey, with a linking balcony that invites pause to breathe in the fragrance of the trees, infusing arrival and departure with a moment completely enveloped in the surroundings. The home has a simple rectangular footprint. Window placement is carefully planned. Windows are placed at the end of a journey, as a focal point, aligned to the views, to invite light in a specific way, or to frame a piece of the land into a wall. Skylights and clerestory windows choreograph the sun and shadows in a constantly changing light show. Large open living spaces flow together at the upper floor—kitchen, dining, family, music—separated by cabinetry, fireplace, or embracing walls. The master suite is acoustically isolated from the rest of the house, the corner of the

SLEEPY HOLLOW

bedroom stripped away and butt glazed, wrapped with thick wood frames to perch the sitting area into the treetops. A freestanding headboard creates the dressing area behind, open yet private, sharing views and volume. Ceilings rise and fall to articulate space and mood. Massive sliding glass doors open the family room and the children's play room onto terraces wrapped with curving perforated aluminum railings. Living spaces are linked by shaped passages washed with light, a folded plane of vertical grain walnut flowing down the stairway to the lower level children's bedrooms, guest rooms, playroom, and study. Sculpted steps connect the lower terrace to a luminous lap pool below. Compositions of cedar siding and contrasting shades of gray stucco lay against each other to accentuate form and texture, all joined with delicate aluminum channels for jewel-like detailing. Walnut cabinetry, concrete and quartzite counters, stainless-steel appliances, glass tile, floating glass sinks, burnished Venetian plaster walls, and hand-blown glass lights complement integrally colored concrete, bamboo, and reclaimed wood flooring. Hand troweling gives rich tone to the concrete floors, blending to the shades of the earth. Though each space reaches outward to connect to the land, the home has a profoundly interior focus on meaningful interaction.

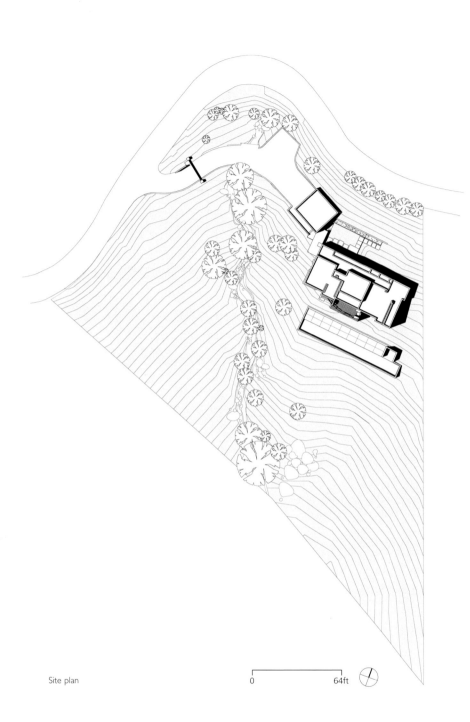

Site plan

0   64ft

Each material, each color, is derived directly from the site; cedar siding matches dry oak leaves, shades of stucco recall the colors of tree bark. The perforated swaths of aluminum railings that sweep in soft curves through the rectilinear forms of the home continue in an undulating line along the driveway, shimmering, almost invisible.

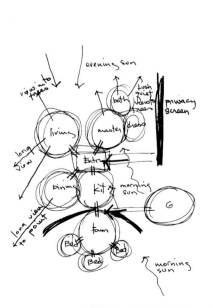

It is possible to stand apart from and be enveloped in one's surroundings at the same time. Windows extrude beyond the walls that hold them toward the elements they are focused on, projecting the inhabitant into the landscape. Two sheets of glass meeting at the corner of the master bedroom dissolve enclosure, allowing the landscape to penetrate the room. What makes us feel embraced or moved, protected or exposed, can be as subtle as a few inches, as spare as an invisible line, as simple as a moment of pause.

The garage and home are separated, tied together by a floating roof slab. Passage between them can be direct or circuitous. Physically, there is room to pause or to step into the dense grove of trees; visually there are choices in the path—to the front door or to the back. It can be uncomfortable entering spaces in which you arrive too immediately. Transitional space, that moment when one is actually between spaces, is profoundly powerful. It gives time to ponder our next step, take a breath, change our mind, or just embrace a moment of calm.

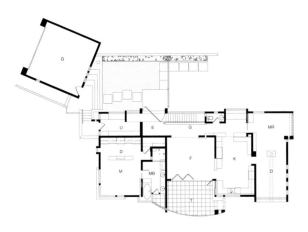

Upper floor

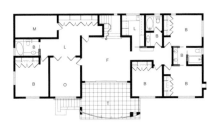

Lower floor

0   16ft

Our first exploratory diagrams trace the sun's path through the days and the seasons. The sun can touch deep into our hearts and warm our souls. The first rays of sunrise bring a new beginning. Many of our clients choose morning as their most important time of day, for this reason. This quote from Ledoux has always been an inspiration: "Establish beautiful masses, present pleasing contrasts, abolish multiple moldings. Lighting effects will offer sufficient variety. The hours of the day and night alone offer so many possibilities. What diversity, when the rising sun spreads its shadows over the earth! What flickering effects when the moon traces labyrinths of light on the building."

Our client spoke of his bath with such poetic, passionate sensitivity that dreams of it permeated my every thought about this home and the implications of each decision. To recognize in his voice the profoundly meaningful renewal he found in his ritual of bathing was paramount and guided so many moves in the design of the whole, attention to each part. In the end it is a tub in the bathroom, its capacity to touch one's soul not immediately apparent. It is of comfortable dimension, wrapped in a soft green concrete embrace, tucked discreetly behind a linen cabinet. It protrudes from the face of the building ever so slightly, enough to wrap three sides with glass. When stepping into the tub he is not yet aware that, on lying down, his body will suddenly be perfectly aligned with the mountain peak. There is great power in these connections with nature. Perhaps that is why so many enduring ancient constructions still fill us with awe. His letter to me after his first bath is what I hope for in my work. All tensions that naturally build during the home's construction were washed away and he was free to begin his new life. If we are to make spaces that truly nurture, there is nothing more important that we, as architects, must protect as the design evolves than the intimate, subtle, unique characteristics of each person whose home is in our hands.

We have spent considerable time living in, studying, and documenting vernacular architecture around the Mediterranean Sea, places that inspire and guide our philosophy and our work. In 1993 we were asked to create the master plan and design the buildings for a new resort community on the Honduran island of Roatán, drawing from this Mediterranean origin. Our first site visit included a single-engine flyover, a slow boat view from the sea, and hiking over the property behind a crew of men hacking through the dense jungle growth with machetes. Parrot Tree Plantation is a unique mixed-use community occupying a 168-acre site of steep hillsides, 3 miles of shoreline, sandy beaches, and two sheltered bays, on the reef-laced waters of the Caribbean Sea. The master plan layout is influenced by villages on the Greek Islands, the Italian and Dalmatian coasts, and hill towns in central Italy and Spain. Commercial spaces and housing are woven into gardens, plazas, and winding roads and walkways. The waterfront promenade, lined with shops, offices, cafes, housing, and pedestrian gathering spaces, is an active, vibrant focal point, embracing a 200-slip, full-service marina. Condominium units include myriad plans for richness and variety in the buildings. Arrangements of the individual units and terraces are articulated to respond to the sun and breezes and to respect views and privacy. Pedestrian movement is filled

PARROT TREE PLANTATION

with twists and turns, infusing surprise in every step, offering places that invite social interaction and foster a sense of community. A murky lagoon has been transformed into a luminous 5-acre turquoise salt-water swimming area surrounded by palm-dotted white powder sand. Private homes line the sandy beaches and climb the hillside above. Beachfront bungalows offer luxurious accommodations that supplement the planned 150-room hotel. An office-reception facility with parking and meeting rooms, a conference center, restaurants, yacht club, sports facilities, health and spa center, and hiking trails through this tropical paradise encompass what has been hailed as one of the most innovative developments in Honduras, receiving the prestigious Copan Award in 2003. Mangrove and swamps have been cleaned, reefs restored, and a nursery provides the palm trees that line beaches and pathways that climb the hillside. Rainwater is collected and purified for drinking; the project treats its own sewage. Rock and coral fragments from the beaches clad building bases and the inclined retaining walls that meander the site, draped in bougainvillea. Colors derive from stones, flowers, leaves, and bark of the local vegetation. Craftsmen from Mexico make the hand-cast brass door hardware, light fixtures, tile murals, stone columns, fountains, and window surrounds. Our studies of enduring environments from around the world have meaningful impact on the places we make ... learning from the past to build the future.

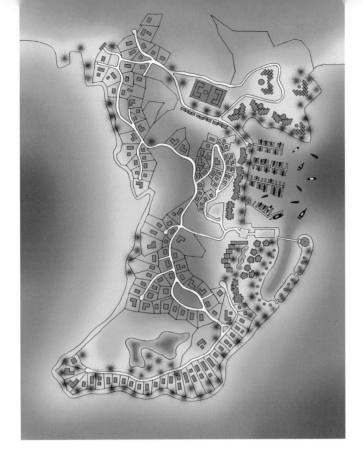

"The sum total of man's created efforts is nowhere more explicitly manifested than in his settlements. Villages, towns and cities, through the arrangement of distinct building types assembled from temporal forms, magnify these human artifacts through repetition, creating images on a superhuman scale. Here too, the world of similitudes guides the ultimate formation, the city taking form almost as though a shadow were taking focus with the shape that cast it." – Nader Ardalan and Laleh Bakhtiar

Symmetry and rhythm give order; spaces unfold. The buildings twist and turn in their relationship to the meanderings of the promenade. Their interaction with the sea, the pedestrians, the inhabitants, takes on richer meaning as they provide places to pause, garden benches on which to sit, a coffee shop, a secret stairway that winds between the buildings and up the hillside. Each living space is individually shaped in relation to the next, terraces are open, yet private, views are broad yet non-invasive. There are essential traditions that are respected, that generate ideas of form and endure in fundamental ways through the ages, but this is a new environment, responsive to the setting, reflecting a philosophy of living that has endured because it is appropriate.

Movement through space is a physical experience that can invite delight in the visual. A meandering path or the tight embrace of a focused descent offer opportunities to experience our surroundings intensely. There can be a sense of calm excitement when attention is directed to the simple pleasure of our path.

A magnificent oak spreads its canopy over a shaded swath of untouched earth, standing beside a mid-century modern home designed with care for its time, in a bold chevron plan. Times change, as do home owners and needs. The young couple that acquired this home found in it a strong beginning, but the outdated materials and room arrangements spoke of a different way of living. They wanted a contemporary home, filled with light, an inviting flow between spaces and elegant details. A new entry procession begins at the street through a steel and stucco gateway, along a tree-lined driveway, arriving at a circular, integrally colored concrete drop-off area, scored in the axial geometries that define new forms. The original entry was uninviting and, once inside, it was low, dark, and confusing as to which way to go. This vestibule was torn open, roofs raised, windows inserted, and walls removed. The experience of passing through a new entry courtyard, past a shimmering steel fountain, a sculpture garden, a contemplation bench, and bridging across a reflecting pool connects more than inside and outside; it connects the

M O R A Q U I T A

past with the future. The new front door, a Mondrian pattern of anigre and ebony woods inlaid with stainless steel, is set on a floating platform of honed golden stone. The new entry gallery glows from broad horizontal bands of glass, a raised ceiling, and clerestory windows. The stone floor, polished inside, terminates at the composed rear wall of the fireplace—a stainless steel box and floating anigre shelf against mottled plaster subtly divided with aluminum channels. To add substance and solidity, walls are thickened, three-dimensional elements float above surfaces, horizontal ledges added that engage and wrap, tying components of the new ideas to the existing building. The floor is ebonized; walls are plastered in mottled tones, or painted in rich colors. New doors and windows invite natural light at every turn. The result is a tangible embrace, a grounding, a sculpting that transforms ephemeral shadows into rich forms. Every space has been re-defined, re-shaped and new finishes have transformed this home into sparkling, light-filled spaces in tune with the new inhabitants and the new era.

We look for moments of pause in the buildings we create, those spaces that are not programmed—the surprises—and in each home they are different. That moment when you are between spaces, between thoughts, between activities—in which you can take a breath, remove your coat, change your mind—is a profound delineation. It is in these between spaces that perception is allowed room to grow.

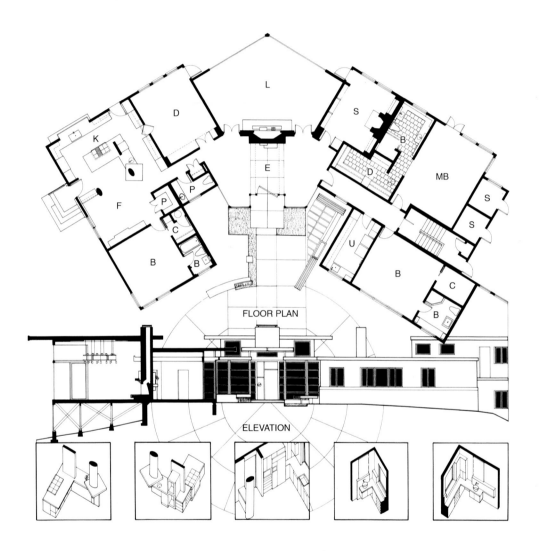

FLOOR PLAN

ELEVATION

Deep-red walls embrace the living room with warmth and tall pairs of glass doors topped with a thick display ledge and new clerestory windows pour natural light into the heart of this home. Steel-troweled plaster wraps around from the entry to engage the fireplace with its floating stainless steel and anigre mantle. The polished golden stone hearth floats above the ebonized floor, suspending the massive wall to complement the hovering steel rings of the chandelier.

The original, outdated kitchen, storage, pantry, and laundry were gutted and re-planned into a large kitchen and an adjacent family sitting area. Elliptical columns clad in black glass mosaic tiles complement the stainless steel and polished granite counters and anigre wood cabinets. Broad windows now showcase the massive oak tree. Thickened walls are plastered and the bar counter raised and skewed, creating a dynamic tension between the kitchen, the bar, and a new family sitting area. Anigre continues into the new master bath, both as cabinets and as deep walls, providing display areas and substance. Texas Brush limestone flows from the floor onto the walls of the new glass shower, and tilted ceramic sinks float on granite counters.

In the dazzling clarity of high plateau air in the desert of central Mexico an abandoned rattan factory sat decaying among ancient trees by the Rio Laja—a 6,000-square-foot warehouse, a 2,000-square-foot shed, and a well. A ceramic artist and a writer saw in these structures the possibilities for a new life. The buildings offered little inspiration, but an alignment to the historic church of Atotonilco cut a compelling angle through the center of the main building and into the well, as did bisecting lines of the second building; and arcs through the buildings' corners all indicated cosmic alignments that suggested mystic meanings and ties to the cosmos. A series of sketches tracing these lines calculated the geometries that shaped space and choreographed movement to form this home. A circuitous driveway winds between earthen mounds, past a new lake, allowing the approach to be a discovery. Buildings appear as though being unveiled by the earth. A meandering footpath continues into the middle of the main building to a massive glass entry door, hinged at the geographic center of the house, the intersecting point of all the geometries. Water trickles down a series of textured walls into a reflecting pool at the entry, water and fire, earth and sky converging to arouse the senses. Living, dining, kitchen, library, office, and master suite each spill onto broad curving terraces, interlocked with steps and railings.

CASA RENACIMIENTO

A long stairway climbs over guest suites to a loft and rooftop mirador with sweeping views to the mountains, tropical thunderstorms, and glorious sunsets. Bi-folding steel and glass doors open the master bedroom to private gardens. Broken mosaic tiles in bold patterns cover the vaulted shower, sliced by a curving glass wall, offering indoor and outdoor showers; an interior garden woven into the dressing area offering a different shower experience. The owner was placed in the rough form of the bathtub for hands to shape its contours to her body and the comfortable position of her elbows for reading. Infinity edges draw an invisible line between water and sky at the lap pool soaring through the gnarled embrace of mesquite branches. The smaller building serves as studio and gallery, a place for discovering the arts of Mexico, the owners' passion for ethnic folk art evident at every niche and wall. Expert craftsmanship is evident in the flowing forms of the windows, doors, and railings made by the blacksmith, in the undulating concrete roofs that link the two structures and provide shade at the dining terrace, in the sculpted ochre, burgundy, and eggplant-colored concrete sinks, in the tile murals, the locally-quarried black stone floors, in the lustrous cabinets, and in the handmade paper, glass, and steel light fixtures. Each hand that formed this home left its mark in the transformation from the ordinary to the extraordinary.

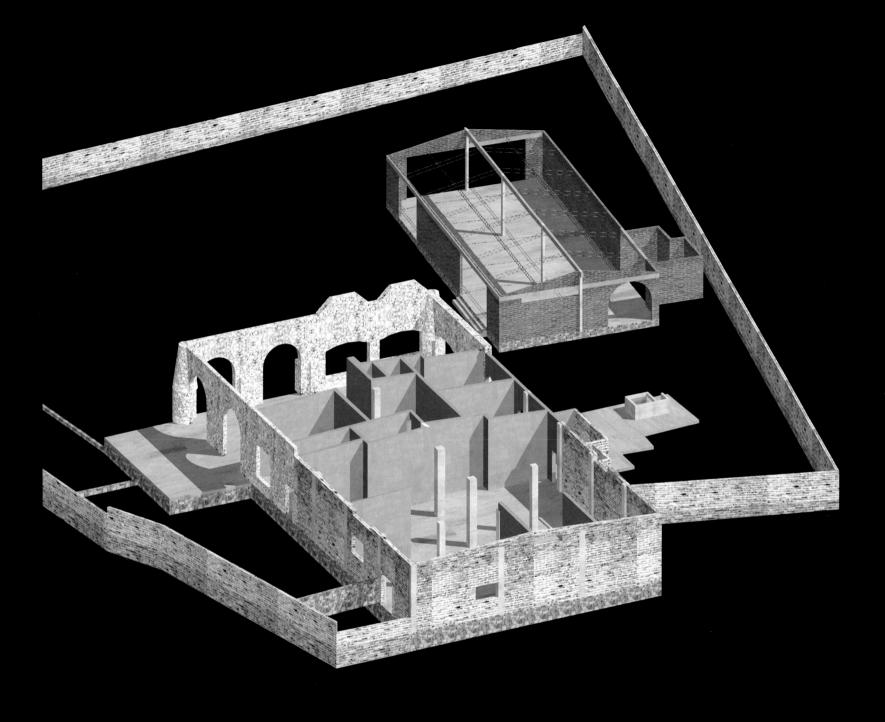

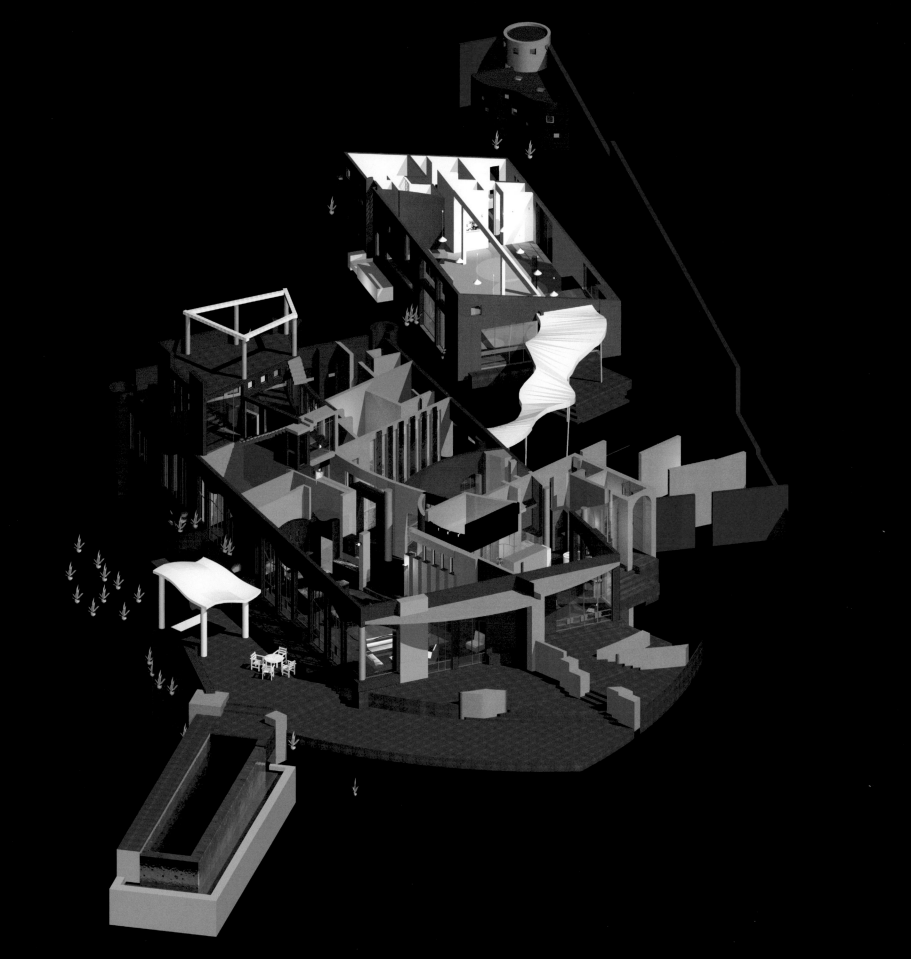

A flowing slab of concrete drapes shade onto the dining terrace. The lap pool flies through ancient mesquite trees, their gnarled reflections submerged in the trembling light of the sky.

Undulating forms offer protection from sun and cast rainwater into a series of temporary sculptures, cascades of shimmering water that appear with the rains. Collected rain is stored in a water tower that overflows through an aqueduct, pausing at a fountain, to feed a new lake. Twenty-foot-tall cylindrical towers envelop guest showers, capped with glass and views to the sky.

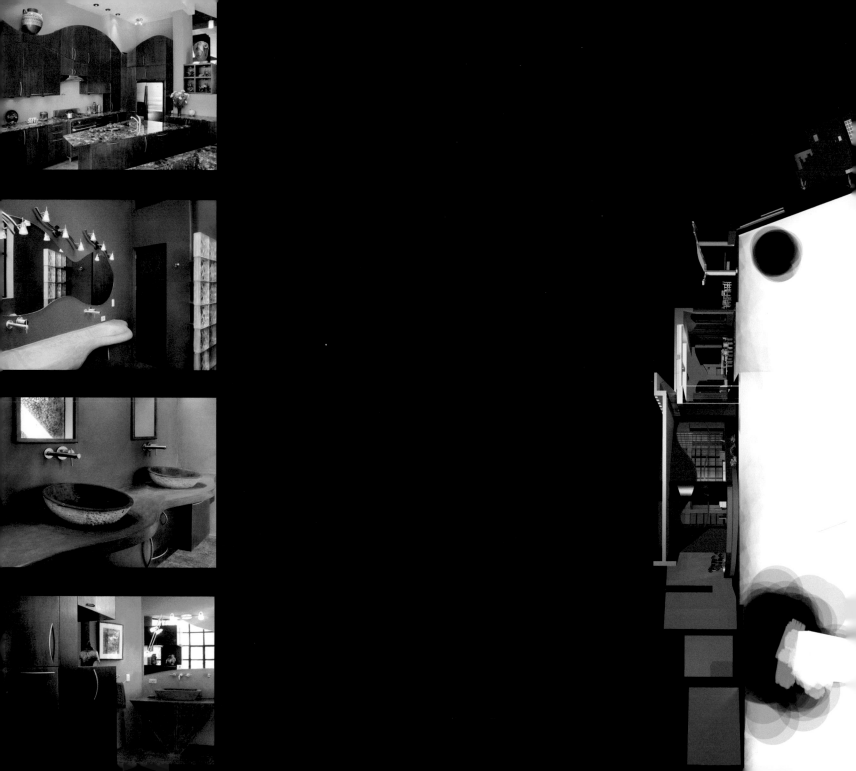

Renacimiento

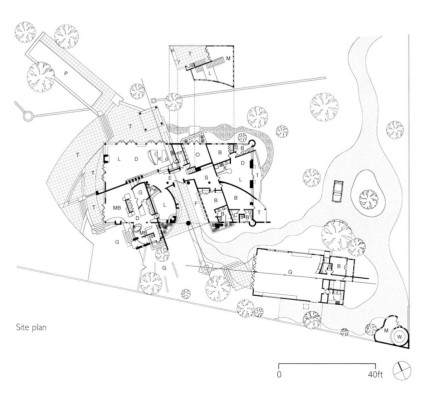

Site plan

Forms reveal themselves in movement, each responding to the organic purpose it serves, geometries deliberately calculated to embrace, surprise, rejoice in the revelation of space. Simple rhythms give way to variegated complexity, layers of shapes and feelings, muted delineation between what we feel and what we do.

Broken tile in shades that derive directly from the vegetation of the site wrap the master shower in voluptuous, organic swaths of color. A curving grid of steel and glass engage the tub and sweep through the shower, dividing and linking inside and out, providing both enclosed and open-air bathing experiences woven visually and spiritually into the fabric of the land. Steps cascade to a private garden, their topography forming places for pause, for momentary meditations.

In a suburban community south of San Francisco where most homes hold tight to the minimum front yard setback, this new home recedes into the center of its site. Nestled into a south-facing slope, it closely guards its privacy while offering a generous garden greenscape to the neighborhood. The large expanse of lawn dotted with birch trees is separated from the home's private gardens by a softly colored cedar wall. A slate walkway leads past a curving black steel fence to a custom front door made of cherry, maple, ebony, and stainless steel, surrounded with translucent glass. Beyond the coffered ceiling at the entry with its pyramidal skylight, a cherry column frames passage into the vaulted living and dining spaces. Living room, dining room, kitchen, sitting area, and the master suite all spill onto a large, curving deck with glass panel railings that disappear against the view and create a sense of flying above the land as it dives into the canyon below. East-facing clerestory windows invite the morning light; wood valences conceal simple mesh shades that block the western sun. Modulated ceiling shapes give definition to and division between spaces that flow together under a

SOUTHDOWN COURT

ceiling of maple paneling. A sweeping stairway with tall windows and a protected view into the gardens leads to secondary spaces below, which open onto a quiet terrace. The fireplace and television are composed together and capped with a cherry mantle. Cherry cabinets and granite counters at the wet bar continue into the kitchen and powder room where they become sculpted pedestals. The kitchen is an inviting place to linger—at the bar or in the adjacent sitting area. With windows on three sides, this room is bathed in natural light. Softly toned limestone and marble complement the serene palette of wood and granite. The crisp form of the house is achieved with tight, vertical cedar siding and integrally colored stucco in shades of taupe. The angle of the roof and the curve of the deck follow the slope and topography of the land. A three-car garage is connected to the house by a covered breezeway through a quiet, protected garden with a sloping stone wall and a specimen Japanese maple tree. In a neighborhood of traditional styles, this home retreats into its gardens, giving more to its community than it demands, quietly, discreetly.

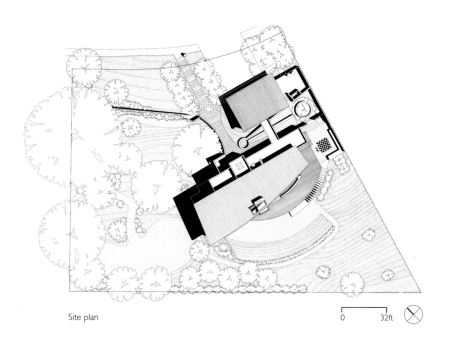

Site plan

0   32ft

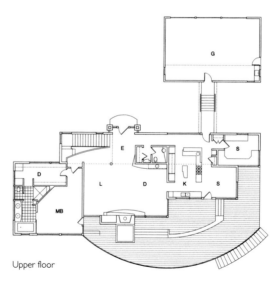

Upper floor

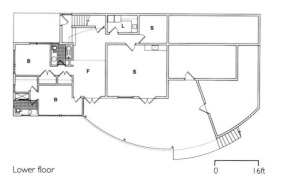

Lower floor

0   16ft

Maple flooring, ceiling, wall panels, entry door, and window frames complement the cherry mantle, column, and details. Frosted glass surrounding the entry door and east-facing clerestory windows invite morning light that casts a golden glow on the rich wood tones. With large windows, fireplace and television each demanding focused attention, black stone cladding unites the fireplace and television into one element rather than two and lets them peacefully disappear when neither is in use.

By eliminating the traditional divisions between rooms, redefining how spaces flow, we open the opportunity for new interaction. A kitchen can become a sitting room, a hall can become a gallery, a stairway a kinetic sculpture; light from one space can illuminate another. When we rethink standard assumptions, even simple things can take on new definition; windows can become glass walls, cabinets can become furniture. Solving a functional requirement offers an opportunity for doing or seeing in a new manner.

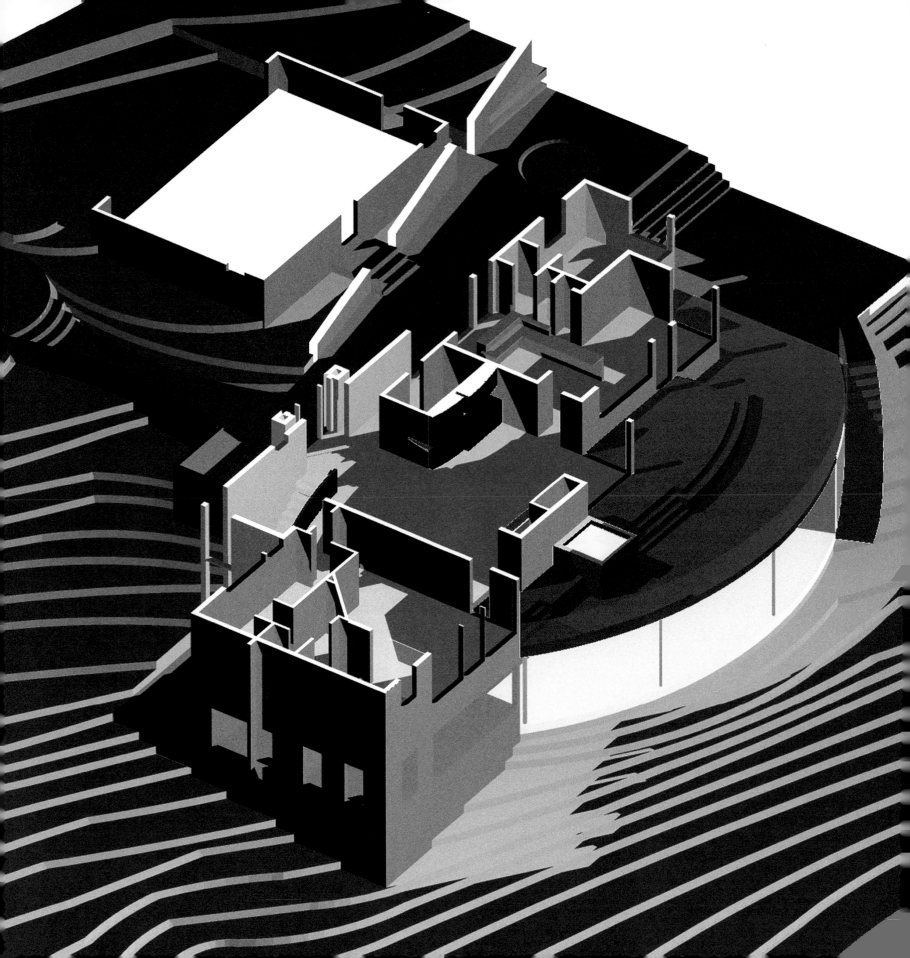

In northern California where times past turned a blind eye to over-grading, a steep hillside was gouged to make way for a home that was badly oriented and poorly constructed. The flat area where it stood for 30 years offered an opportunity that would not be possible now, in times more sensitive to preservation of natural grades. Rather than placing this new home where the old had been, it was pushed to the edge of the slope to wrap around a level garden/courtyard that fills this home with light and outdoor life. For a young family with twin baby girls, a home on one level with protected outdoor space and plenty of room for play was the right plan. The upper hillside gently slopes into the courtyard and the lower hillside falls away below rooms that float above the land. Stretched into a long slender U shape, most of this home is one room wide, offering broad views through wide expanses of glass to Mount Tamalpais on one side, and into the sheltered courtyard on the other. Sunlight washes across the terraced slope with lush gardens and a sculpted walkway to a spa overlooking the courtyard. A tower, whose inverted butterfly roof frames the mountain peak, contains the baby grand piano and becomes the vestibule to the private wing where a master suite, two children's

RIDGECREST

bedrooms, a bathroom, and utility rooms are oriented at 90 degrees to the public wing. Axial alignments invite twists and turns in the paths of daily life, a window framing the landscape at the visual end of every passage, with myriad invitations to pause, linger, or change course along the way. Sculpted walls and changes of material and ceiling height define spaces that flow together, intimate or open, depending on the activities. Tightly spaced cedar siding and integrally colored stucco layer against each other in contrasting textures, colors drawn from the surrounding vegetation. Thickened red stucco walls frame portals to the lush courtyard, a wide ribbon of water spilling into a cool fountain, sending ripples of sound and reflections of light. Built-in storage, bar, walk-in pantry, and closets accommodate the paraphernalia of life in spaces that are serene and spare. Cherry cabinetry in the kitchen and living room, floating vanities of beech and cherry in the master bath, granite and limestone counters, hand-blown glass pendant lights, and stainless steel appliances complement multi-tonal slate and bamboo flooring, each material wrapping a warm embrace around the inhabitants, comforting in its function in this receptacle of life.

A meandering concrete and slate walkway leads through a landscaped garden to the maple, cherry, and sandblasted glass front door protected with a steel and glass canopy. Living spaces spill onto decks with transparent glass railings. Soft washes on cedar siding, strong shades of stucco, iridescent bronze metal roofing—each color derived from the site—work together to create a home that is bold, yet comfortable in its natural setting.

Portals are the connections, the transition point from one place to another. Sometimes they are boldly marked, as in the portal between inside and out. At other times they are more subtle, as in the portal between stress and calm, that may come in the form of the gentle sound of water in a fountain, or the portal between exposed and protected, as in movement from an open to a contained view.

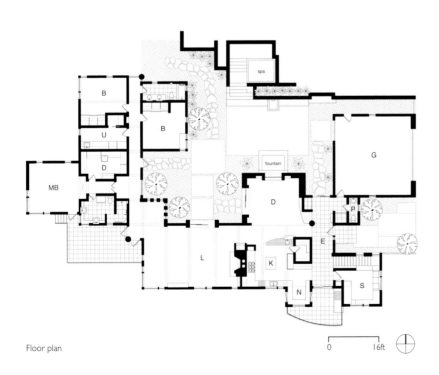

Floor plan

0   16ft

A red stucco column in the entry frames passage into high vaulted living spaces with rhythmic, wood beams giving definition to open-plan living. Clerestory windows capture north light and large glass doors to the courtyard bathe the interior in a natural glow. Golden colored stucco is sculpted into a masonry fireplace dividing the living room from the kitchen and containing niches and cabinets for stereo equipment and art objects.

Natural materials bring warmth and comfort into the spaces they inhabit. Cherry, bamboo, laminated beams, blown glass, stone, plaster—each carries its own luminescent qualities, and each is complementary to the colors of nature framed in every window.

In the beautiful Mexican town of San Miguel de Allende, in a quiet, traditional neighborhood, a modest home with small rooms and low ceilings sat on a 25-by-60-foot lot. The owner acquired the adjacent property with the intent of enlarging and opening up his home. Existing rooms were gutted and re-planned with rooms in the addition to include a new living room, a new master suite, a garage, and a studio. Existing gardens at the front and rear and the configuration of the existing rooms led to an expansion of the idea of a home wrapped with gardens and terraces. A new stone wall at the street sets the world within apart, a world of sculpted, flowing spaces that sparkle with natural light. The existing kitchen and powder room were gutted and replanned to link the new and old. The original long, narrow living room was divided into uncomfortable halves by an existing concrete beam at the ceiling. To unify the space and transform it into a dramatic dining room, the beam was wrapped in wood and 12 additional "beams" were added to create a low, warm embrace around a new 14-foot-long dining table

FRANCISCO MARQUEZ

and gardens at each end of the room. A concrete hearth, thick walls, deep-set niches, and floor-to-ceiling glass create strong, spacious rooms. Glass-block walls glisten under high ceilings, or are individually set in thick walls to offer privacy and cast sparkles of light as the sun moves through the seasons. Brick domes and vaults (*bovedas*) are a specialty of the region, beautiful hand constructions made without formwork or guidelines. Traditional Mexican tile flooring is washed with a deep-rose stain to add depth and complexity to the color, with a scattering of decorative deep-purple accent tiles. Integrally colored concrete in ochre and burgundy is burnished smooth, the natural mottling giving warmth and life to the touch on counters, columns, benches, and sinks. Handmade pine cabinets and furniture are aniline-dyed a deep burgundy. Soft shades of plum and sage green with accents of deep turquoise on the walls were inspired by the owner's art collection. Furniture, light fixtures, tile murals, gardens, and custom elements designed for this home are handmade by local skilled and devoted craftsmen, a large part of the joy for us in working in this very special place.

From the street a new rugged half-inch stone wall with a deeply set entry door of thick pine timber laced into a wooden grid protects this home. Inside, a 15-foot-tall grid of glass invites passage through an entry garden into the new living room, another grid of glass opposite, open to a rear garden, terrace, and a small orchard of citrus trees.

A brick dome over the living room soars to 18 feet, the room wrapped in tall glass walls that open to gardens front and rear. The new kitchen, open with a bar counter to the living and through an art niche to the dining, overlooks the rear gardens. Quiet and private, the new master suite sits level with the old roof, with terraces off each side to invite sun and offer views in every direction. Another brick dome soars above the bedroom and thick walls are carved into deep windowsills, a headboard for the bed and a two-sided fireplace to the bathtub beyond.

Second floor before

Second floor after

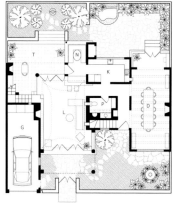

First floor before

First floor after   0   16ft

Aniline dye on the 10-foot-tall bedroom door and bath cabinets is luminescent in a deep-wine color, which continues in the rich tones of hand-polished concrete that shapes the tub and forms deep sills and ledges that wrap into the shower as a long bench. A two-sided fireplace links the bedroom with the tub that has been hand-shaped to the owner's body dimensions. The bath and master entry are topped with a brick vault that spans above walls and over the serpentine stair. A multicolored tile mural at the shower wall continues on the floor and into the tub.

Eight luxurious condominiums stand on a narrow slice of tropical beach on the Honduran Island of Roatan in the Caribbean, where sparkling white sands host deep-orange sunsets over turquoise waters. As is true with most waterfront developments, the program called for minimum unit width, maximum vista, and maximum privacy. Unfortunately, many units in waterfront developments wind up with a living–dining kitchen to the view, a central bedroom and two baths without windows, and a bedroom at the rear on a public walkway, which precludes the possibility of privacy. The site for this project was exceptionally deep, offering the opportunity to stagger the units sufficiently to visually and psychologically separate them, providing considerable privacy. The site's depth also offered the possibility for development of an interior courtyard within each unit—"outdoor rooms" that pour natural light into the center of the unit, even into the hallway of the adjacent unit through scatterings of glass blocks. Lower units contain living, dining, kitchen, and two bedrooms; upper units have a third bedroom in a lofty overlook and dining rooms with 18-foot ceilings. Living spaces spill onto broad

C O R A L   S A N D S

terraces that overlook the beach and the sea in two directions, wrapped in massive two-story frames that diffuse the scale of the building. Luxurious kitchens have large windows directly to the view and central dining rooms and master bedrooms open into the courtyards. All bathrooms have windows and interior glass-block walls, infusing them with light. Individual stairways serve each of the upper units, assuring privacy as no neighbor is ever walking past. The rear façades are articulated with different window configurations at each room to confuse and delight the eye, avoiding monotonous repetition and offering the rear bedrooms unrestricted views to the mountains. By providing interior courtyards in these units, every space is filled with natural light and open, private access to the outdoors. Shadows play against bright colors that derive from and complement the tropical vegetation. Stucco walls, ribbons of aluminum railings with a bronze patina, high-fire ceramic floor tiles, and dense granites help to weather the salty environment.

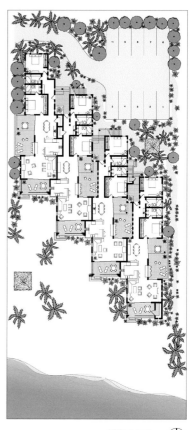

Site plan

0   30ft

A cascade of monumental frames wrap terraces focused on this perfect view. The building unfolds, each unit with its private slice of tropical paradise. There is a stillness that comes with isolation, a peace and connectedness to the moment, the texture of the ripples in the water, the glimmers of sunlight shimmering through waves, the luminous glow as the sun washes the sky.

"It is not so much what you see, but what you feel. You feel the reflection of something, it is beautifully stated. It reflects something you would like to expend the expression of, although you may not know its background. It transcends the knowledge about it. You see it and you feel that you must see it. It is the kind of thing that you would not see in nature without man. It spells an association of man to man. It spells civilization." – Louis Kahn

What color is light? Is it that golden glow we see at midday, that red of the sunset? Is the light we see in shadows actually light in another form or is it something altogether different? Every moment of the day the life of light changes and with each change can touch our souls anew and fill us with overwhelming gratitude for even the simplest things that surround us.

250

A tiny, worn apartment at the ground floor level behind the garage and storage rooms of a San Francisco Marina District three-unit building begged to be re-thought and re-finished, the program calling for transformation from a studio to a one-bedroom apartment. The design approach often taken when the area to work with is very limited, is to assume that the individual spaces within must, therefore, be small, and that there is no room for areas deemed expendable, such as an entry, a work area, a separate dining area. Rather than beginning this project with the idea that, since there was so little space to start with, some areas must be diminished to make others seem more spacious, we took the opposite approach—that each individual area must be as generous as possible so that the whole would feel larger and more gracious. New space was captured inch by inch—by lowering the floor to heighten the ceiling, reworking framing to eliminate intrusive elements, increasing the size of windows and doors, and edging into an adjacent storage area. Working closely with our client, a multi-talented designer whose career has included real estate, interior design, specialty finishes, and most recently, her highly acclaimed home makeover television program in England, *House Doctor*, resulted in a most interesting collaboration. Despite its small size, this cramped studio apartment has been completely

GOLDEN GATE

transformed into a spacious, comfortable one-bedroom apartment that includes a living room with separate work area, a generous kitchen with large island, a bedroom with a large closet and dresser, a gracious bathroom with an extra-long tub as well as a formal entry with a wide sideboard. An intruding foundation wall has been capped with a wood top to become a long display ledge and side table in the living area, adding sculptural mass and dimension. A transformable piece of custom furniture changes easily from a work center with ample storage into a formal dining table when the island eating area is insufficient. A thickened wall with open shelving supports translucent sliding panels to divide the living room from the bedroom. The new 8-foot square sliding glass doors and large window open the space to the rear garden, filling it with light. San Francisco's temperate climate invites expanded living onto the wood deck overlooking the rear garden. Luminescent red glass mosaic tile on the kitchen wall, charcoal-gray laminate counters, and stainless steel detailing complement shimmering bamboo cabinetry and flooring. Placed at 45 degrees for added dimension, the sustainable bamboo flooring is reminiscent of California grasses. The blend of natural maple, bamboo, rice paper, and luscious glass tiles with crisp glass, laminate, and stainless steel, and the soft, bright colors of the walls provide an earthy, sensual, clean background for the contemporary furnishings and art in this intimate environment.

Rather than eliminate a foyer, this small apartment boasts a 6-foot-long sideboard at a generous entry area with an aluminum and ribbed glass door. A steel frame atop the island cabinet, which also hides the television, supports a floating glass counter.

A large soaking tub with a deep niche elongating the space feels anything but small. The wide maple counter at the bathroom vanity and an artful linen cabinet are washed with halogen light, the walls wrapped in multi-toned glass mosaic tile. The half-height wall separating the sleeping and living areas provides bedroom shelving topped with translucent shoji panels for privacy. Adjacent backlit panels transform the closet into a glowing light fixture. The bed is tucked into a niche, adding both dimension and serenity to a petite but comfortable space.

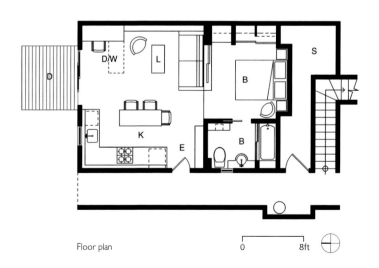

Floor plan

0   8ft

North of San Francisco where the land rolls in straw-colored hills dotted with gnarled oaks and rocky outcroppings, shadows are sharp and colors glow in the clarity of California sunlight. Two rectangular forms sit askew, hinged with a raw concrete column, intersected with a cylindrical tower, geometry interlocking the forms. Overhanging roofs are braced with red steel struts. Earthen shades of stucco spring from the land. A teacher and a computer programmer moved to the Bay Area from Seattle for new work and a new life. Their passionate involvement in the project even included our client wiring the home himself. The plan is simple, open, all of the parts united around a sculptural stairway. Movement is celebrated in the compositional arrangements of the components. There is serenity in the simplicity of the program and in the interdependent linking of the forms. Spaces flow both horizontally and vertically, around the central stairway and up it, physically in function, and visually in contemplation from several vantage points. The dominant lines of the living area flow through the adjacent, angled volume to create a dynamic interaction between the private spaces above and their container.

RINCON RIDGE

Limestone flooring is soft and cool in the warm climate. Cherry and maple are bound with steel and stone in cabinets and steps. The garage is separated from the home, connected with a trellised path to symbolically and physically tie the owners to their land each time they arrive or depart. A curved terrace ties the building components together in a calm link between inside and out. Preservation of existing trees allows this home to sit peacefully among them and they, in turn, provide privacy from nearby neighbors. The angle of the roofs reflects the slope of the land, the struts reflect the branches in the trees; the shadows and orientation align with the sun. All organic ties spring directly from this particular piece of land. Architectural forms are archetypal—cylinder and shed. The rhythms of the exposed beams are classical. The scale of the columns and thickness of walls are monumental. These are traditional elements, all drawn from great respect for why those traditions endure, but assembled in a new way to make a building that speaks of its place and its time, and of those who inhabit it.

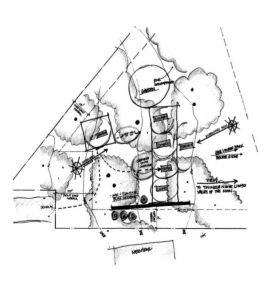

Second floor

First floor

0   16ft

Cherry and black granite wrap the kitchen in a warm embrace, tall windows overlooking the front garden. The cylindrical dining nook becomes a quiet retreat from the open-plan living; thick walls with an art niche and contained views to the rear yard make a place that feels apart, protected.

The master bedroom is enveloped in cherry and maple cabinetry, crisp with slender aluminum reveals. The headboard divides the bedroom from the bathroom, eliminating the need for walls, the angle of the bed adding privacy and detachment from the public spaces below. Luminous green tiles and jade slate on the floor wrap the master bath in the color of water. Sunlight streaks in through a carefully placed skylight. Tucked into a private, meditative space, the deep cylindrical soaking tub is skylit and sparkling from a wall of glass blocks.

In the arid landscape of high plateau desert in central Mexico, this home stands in startling contrast to its surroundings, yet it is formed by and in complete harmony with its setting. Aligned on a north/south axis, the building sits slightly skewed on its suburban lot in a gated community of traditional homes. This skew opened the opportunity for gardens all around and orients rooms to the sun and mountains, casting views past nearby houses rather than toward them. A long, axial walkway leads from the street, climbing a few steps, past a mesquite tree, to a large glass door flanked by tall walls that protect and focus movement. The home is a series of interconnected vertical and horizontal planes of concrete, rooms created by glass enclosure, separated into two buildings, public and private, connected by the central passage. Living, dining, and kitchen occupy the first building, entirely open under a 4.5-meter (14-foot, 9 inch) ceiling. The living room is separated from the dining/kitchen area by a level change and a low, built-in cabinet. A massive skylight continues the line of the central axis, wood beams casting shadows that delineate the movement of the sun. A thickened wall is carved with niches for art and a fireplace. Floor-to-ceiling windows complement large glass doors that open unexpectedly with pivot hinges set at the third point. Concrete counters flow through tall windows to form

PALO COLORADO

a built-in barbeque area. The master suite is isolated by seemingly solid walls that dissolve into a sweep of glass with long vistas over a sagebrush-strewn landscape to violet mountains. The bedroom floor extrudes east through the glass wall to become a terrace, magnifying the depth of the vista, completely open, yet private by orientation and flanking walls. The master bath is designed as a sculpture of concrete planes that climb and spill from counters to seats and into a deep tub, out a wall-to-wall window into a private garden. The guest suite is tucked quietly behind thickened walls. There is simplicity in the plan that invites poetic contemplation of the setting, at once completely integrated into the land, yet distinctly separated. The muted purples, oranges, and ochres of the landscape are amplified in the colors of the walls, laying against each other in monumental compositions that unfold with movement, embrace, and pause. Ceilings are soft green, floors deeper greens drawn from the agaves, sagebrush, and cactus that thrive in this region. Spaces are revealed gradually, by surprise, bound by focused geometries. There is a spiritual pull to discover what lies behind the walls, and an invitation to pause in each space. Constantly changing light imbues this home with a translucent tie to the cosmos. This is a home born of the land, set apart by its boldness, yet enveloped intimately by its surroundings, harmony in the forms washed with light.

first **thoughts**

walls to invite
walls to contain
walls to frame
walls to open

walls to keep privacy
in

street

house

wall

writing studio

a central **garden**, heart of your **home**

divides public from private

invites passage and pause

your world within the larger world

with each step new vistas are **revealed**

...that which was **hidden** unfolds

infused with **light**

responsive to the
rising and setting
of the sun

shaped to link that
which is
without
to that
which is
within...

simple forms made **powerful**
by their very simplicity

a seamless connection between you and the
earth

a container for your lives in this **new**
world

vibrant **color**

clarifies
shapes
defines
links
makes sculpture of the simplest **form**

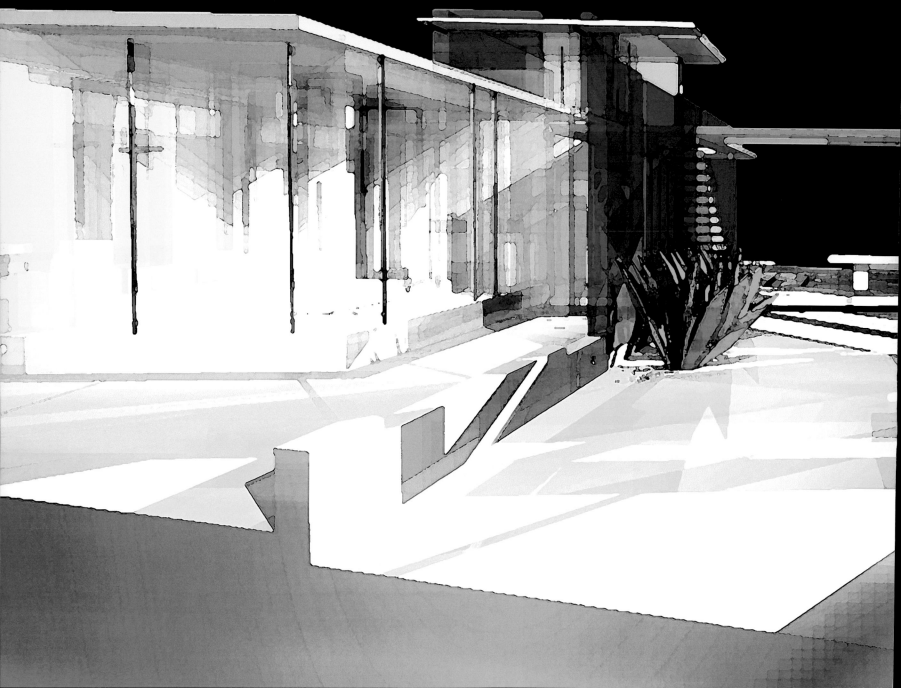

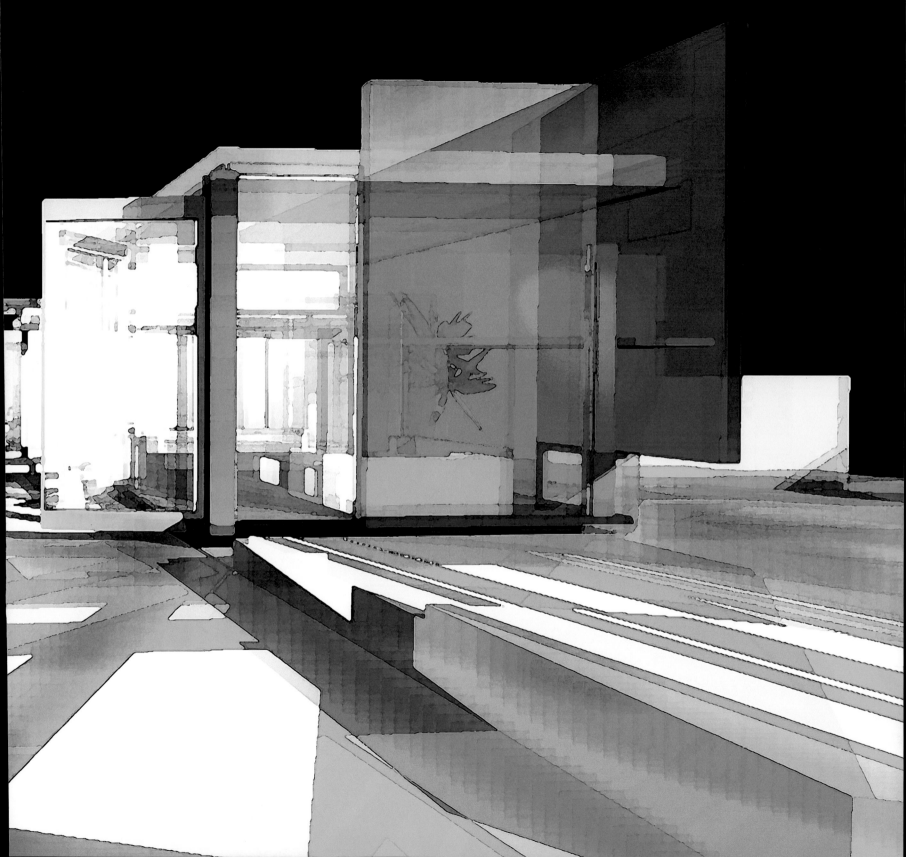

"The true work of architecture is not a monument, but a receptacle of life, a construction that lives close to its creator, following him in the various, changing functions of his life, to each of which it lends a certain form, a form that is never finished or final, but that is completed as time goes by, flowering again and again into daily perfection, because it is born and re-born not a being, but a becoming… The painter Leger once said: *Architecture is not art, it is a natural function. It grows out of the ground like animals and plants, or like a tree that unfolds and develops, as long as the man who planted it tends it with proper care.*" – Aris Konstantinidis

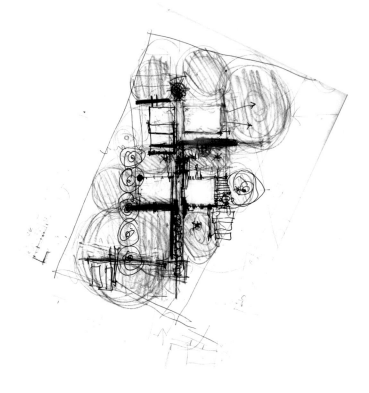

Second floor

First floor

0   16ft

Engaging the Human Spirit

By Philip Enquist

It is difficult to argue against the proposition that beautiful and vibrant cities are among the most powerful proofs of civilization's greatness. Unfortunately, today we confront the equally valid proposition that it is difficult to find architecture that enables the harmonious and effortless relationship of buildings to the land they occupy and to the communities they are supposed to serve. In this era of "McMansions," monster family rooms, quadruple garages, and mega kitchens, we hunger for a more sensitive and intelligent approach to home design.

When we discover architecture that is respectful of the land, that possesses an understanding of the relationship between city and structure, and that is in scale with its surroundings, great praise is due. The equation is as simple as it is powerful: cities need great architects to renew the built environment as much as great architects need exceptional cities in which to frame their work.

Simply, Steven and Cathi House are just such exceptional architects. Their art—for House + House homes and other designs are nothing less than art—recognizes and realizes what it is to work within the context of, and improve, urban life. Even the name of their firm, "House + House," could not be a happier shorthand for what they do—create soul-stirring houses and other projects defined by a clear, nurturing, and tranquil relationship to the environment and the soul. A House + House project will enclose and define space in rich textures. It will rise from the ground with volumes of intense color. It will reach out to and incorporate sunlit days and velvet nights.

The Houses focus on the elements of design that energize them. These include color, form, texture, and the relationship to the surroundings, mixed with craftsmanship, local materials, and a unique sense of space and light. Their work says to us: "Architecture should inspire. It should provide a sense of emotion. It should demonstrate a commitment to craftsmanship. It should, above all, embrace one's soul." These are clearly not easy or facile principles to guide one's work. Yet they are the essence of the sensibility capable of evoking the passion and emotion of architecture that inspires one's everyday life and is at the heart of the Houses' efforts.

Working closely with local artisans, Cathi and Steven House display a knack for discovering distinctive materials that celebrate the indigenous. Passionate, anchored in tradition, and rooted to place, House + House designs are at the same time soaring, light-filled, and emotion provoking. A House + House home mirrors its owner's desire for a beautiful life, for a positive relationship with the surroundings, and for a series of spaces that are ultimately life renewing. Architecture by House + House can be reminiscent of the serenity of Luis Barragán, of the colors of Ricardo Legoretta, of the beauty of William Turnbull, and the playfulness of Charles Moore.

From the street a House + House project can be discreet, quiet, and humble. Entering that home, however, a remarkable journey begins; spaces unfold, volumes emerge, colors wash over the visitor in ways that approach the mystical. Surprises occur at every stage of that voyage; preconceived notions are shattered, reinvented, and reinterpreted. An outdoor entry court can become a living room, a rooftop, a secret garden, a bathroom, or a lantern for an adjacent porch at night.

Many of these houses have a combination of form and color that will bring to mind the great mid-20th-century modern artists such as Henri Matisse, Alexander Calder, or Paul Klee. There is something about the Houses' choices of color and form that evokes this celebrated era. Perhaps it is the deep reds, cerulean blues, faded rose, warm grays, and rich ochre yellows. Perhaps it is the bold crescent forms in the stone paving, or the handrails that scroll up flights of stairs.

Renowned Chicago-based architect Margaret McCurry has asked a critical question: "How does one develop the sensibility needed to elevate the enclosing of space or the molding of form into an aesthetic act?" In the case of Steven and Cathi House, the answer has most to do with an artistic sensibility that is an inspiration to those of us who endeavor to direct city development toward enhanced livability. Their work is poetic, insightful, and intelligent. It is influenced not by trends or fashion, but rather by views, climate, culture, light and shadow, and certainly by the desire to inspire. The work of House + House can offer motivation to a profession that needs to find ways to create places of unique beauty, inspiration, and influence. Ultimately, their projects call to mind a quote by Mexico's great writer, poet and diplomat, Octavio Paz, who celebrated architectural space "solid without heaviness and tied to the earth but with a desire for flight."

In their work House + House are accomplishing just such a soaring architectural poetry. How wonderful then, in this world of facile lifestyles, global economies, and leadenly similar transnational architecture, that the two Houses are working slowly, carefully, and artfully as painters, sculptors, and architects do, to craft buildings that engage the human spirit and enrich the soul.

Philip Enquist, FAIA, Planning Partner
Skidmore Owings & Merrill, Chicago

Light Movement Embrace

By Cathi House

Making a home is an intensely personal experience, inviting us to know each new client intimately and to discover the potential of each piece of land—these alone are powerful inspirations. We design homes, intimate receptacles for lives, families, and dreams. It is a delicate task to create a building worthy of that function: taking concrete, steel, wood, and stone and molding them as efficiently as possible into the stuff dreams are made of, into places that might touch someone's soul.

We look to our travels as one of our greatest sources of inspiration and personal growth. It is during our travels that we have learned to observe the unspoken, see the world with open eyes, let go of preconceptions, and explore new ways of thinking. We are renewed in our work, our vision, and re-ground ourselves in the nature of spaces we want to make. Steven and I met on our first day of architecture school, married four years later and worked in Philadelphia, saving for a year-long voyage through Europe. We didn't know as we began that journey what an odyssey of discovery it would become, that it would be our journey into awareness. Many extraordinary experiences opened our minds to possibilities previously unimagined, spinning our lives onto a path we could not have designed or even dreamed of, a path that changed us forever and influences our work every day. The fates do, sometimes, weave a path for our lives more wondrous than we could design for ourselves, if we are open to the possibilities. What a wonderful word—*possibilities*—to allow events to unfold, to appreciate the path of discovery. Light, movement, embrace, composition, proportion, focus, vista, color, texture, touch, reflection, pause, glimpse, surprise, wonder, and joy are some of our tools and we find great pleasure in discovering how to craft them in a unique manner for each project.

Light is the first generator as we begin the design process, a formidable presence, one that can be very harsh and invasive if not properly respected. Our first diagrams track the sun through the days and the seasons, to guide us in orienting spaces on a site—the morning sun shining into a breakfast room, the dining room aligned to the sunset. As the design develops, the intimacies of the sun's touch become details, inviting it to caress, to warm or cool, to surprise, to sparkle—as in the patterns of light from a skylight, or strong shadows cast by sculpting, or walls that glow as though illuminated from within, even how a beam of light can become one of the inhabitants of the home interacting with the building and its occupants in a living, changing embrace. Light has the power to make solid material glow as though translucent, to reflect a color from one place to another, to catch us by surprise, to fill our days with wonder. There is an insightful thought from the great architect Louis Kahn, which has always been an inspiration to us: "Material which was derived from light was spent light. Spent light was a material which cast a shadow by the grace of light, and the shadow belonged to the light. Silence met light. Light, the giver of all presence."

Movement is the second generator in our design process, a tool that we learned while living in small villages of the Mediterranean, places that we have returned to again and again to refine our understanding. Wandering village paths revealed to us the idea that space can be choreographed, that our surroundings and the paths through them can have profound effect on how we feel—excitement, anticipation, awareness of something about to unfold, startled by the power in a shaft of sunlight raking a textured wall, moved by the glow of color that becomes tangible at twilight. Our hearts have been touched by the poetry of a carefully placed window, in movement through a perfectly proportioned, sculpted space. We learned to see, not just with our eyes, but with our souls. Movement through those villages is the most literal way we bring an idea forward, so that how you move through and around our buildings has that quality of surprise, focus, distraction … so that the dances of daily life have that richness of movement—for if a space is well-conceived it will touch and delight, arouse those intimate reactions that come from deep inside ourselves.

Embrace is one of the most important qualities that a building—a home in particular—should provide. Home is a refuge, a place that holds family and dreams. There is of course the real embrace—as in a courtyard or walls that wrap—but embrace can be subtle, even invisible, and yet still tangible, as in the proportions of a room, the comfort of a color, the solidity of construction, the depth of a shadow, even by a large swath of glass—if it is well-placed in the wall to bring forth that sense of protection rather than exposure. To wrap a building around its inhabitants in an intimate embrace that allows worries to slip away and hopes to come forward is the most powerful contribution an architect can make in their design.

Just as the shape of our community reflects our culture, our history, our values, our place in the world, so our homes reflect who we are as individuals, our dreams, our fears, our innermost selves. The environment we create is a mirror of who we are and we can shape our environment to help us become who we wish to be, both as people and as part of the larger community of man. We use steel, concrete, stone, and myriad other materials, both natural and manmade, and we have a philosophical choice in how they are assembled—whether guided by the heart and poetic possibilities, concern for the environment, technology, sustainability … and, once formed, they clearly express in the reality of that stone and steel—both the obvious and the underlying motivations behind their creation.

Buildings are static, fixed in time, in place, in form, yet we experience them in a dynamic way that can bring them to life, and they, in turn, can invite us to experience amazement, pleasure, and wonder. We move through buildings physically, of course, but in so many other ways that reflect who we are, what is happening in our lives. Depending on our state of mind, our movement may be spiritual, emotional, visual … Our bodies and our senses are the tools that give energy to buildings. As we move through or around them they change, forms lay against each other in constantly changing configurations, we are pulled, invited, embraced, set at ease, our curiosity engaged, satisfied. How we experience buildings can transform concrete into poetry and touch us as deeply as a magnificent sunset. It is our hope that in the buildings we make we are able to transform life's daily activities to richly-felt, breathless moments, in environments that celebrate each life experience.

Life is a journey.

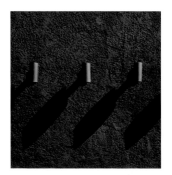

L I G H T

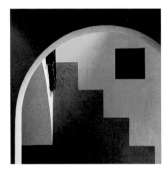

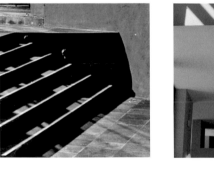

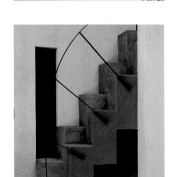

M O V E M E N T

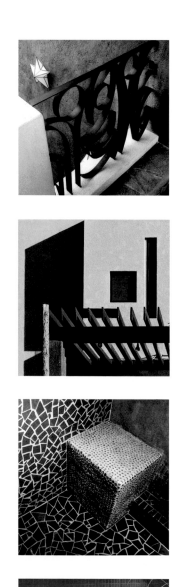

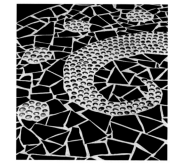

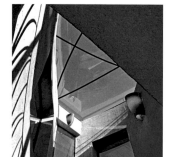

E M B R A C E

Firm Profile

For 26 years House + House Architects have crafted intimate, personal architecture. Cathi and Steven House endeavor to create beauty, serenity, and awe in their work. Their greatest inspiration comes from the subtleties of each site and the deepest recesses of their client's souls. Through intimate analysis, they mold each project into a unique, magical, and harmonious environment. The poetic quality of their work derives from simple things—the magic sparkle of sunlight raking across a textured wall, the harmony of perfect proportion, the joy of movement along a well-choreographed path … Deeply sensitive to form, color, texture, light, and movement, House + House create a tangible spirit within each home, molded to the process of living. Committed to sustainability, their work focuses on enduring design that incorporates natural light and ventilation, passive solar heating, grey/rain water systems, local and recycled materials, shading, high-efficiency glazing and mechanical systems, and development of microclimates and strong connections to the outdoors.

With Cathi and Steven House, architecture does indeed seem like a natural function. They met as architecture students at Virginia Tech in 1970 and married four years later. Products of a unique education at Virginia Tech's College of Architecture, which emphasized design at all scales and the inter-relatedness of all forms of art and architecture, they began House + House Architects in 1982 with the full array of practical and theoretical tools at their command. House + House have produced a diverse body of work reflecting their passion for site-specific, well-choreographed buildings in California, Florida, Hawaii, Mexico, and the Caribbean. In 1989 *Architecture* magazine featured House + House in their "Discovery Issue" on emerging talent. Since then, they have received more than 50 design awards and their work has been featured in numerous national and international publications including their first monograph, *House + House Architects: Choreographing Space*. Cathi and Steven have lectured extensively around the United States and Mexico, serve on the Advisory Council for the School of Architecture + Design at Virginia Tech and are working to establish a new Architecture Study Abroad Program based in Mexico.

Dedicated to continuing their own education through travel, Cathi and Steven acknowledge the profound influence their exposure to cultures around the world has had on their professional work. For more than 30

years they have traveled extensively throughout Europe, Asia, and Latin America documenting vernacular architecture. As young architects, they lived in Greece where they discovered indigenous architecture and their souls as architects were formed. Their stunning book, *Mediterranean Villages: An Architectural Journey,* celebrates their investigations of villages throughout the Mediterranean—the hill towns of central Italy, the Aegean Islands of Greece, the Dalmatian coast, and the Andalusian region of southern Spain. Recorded in fascinating drawings, indelible black-and-white photographs, and a text of fortified research punctuated with quotations from a wide array of Mediterranean observers, this book is a record both of the unforgettable landscapes they have visited and their own development as architects and artists dedicated to understanding and embracing the human spirit.

In 1989, while searching for a stone quarry in Mexico, Cathi and Steven discovered the historic colonial town of San Miguel de Allende in the Central Highlands north of Mexico City. That was the beginning of a love affair with a place that has offered them new opportunities in the refinement of their craft. They built a home for themselves in San Miguel in 1993 and have since designed over 17 houses in central Mexico and on the Sea of Cortez. With offices in San Francisco and San Miguel de Allende they divide their time between both worlds, each reinforcing and supporting the other.

Selected Bibliography

AIA. *The American House—Design for Living*, The AIA Press & The Images Publishing Group, 1992, pp. 24–27.

Anderson, Grace. "On a Windy Hill", *Architectural Record*, May 1990, p.27.

Balint, Juliana. "L'Essenzialita Moltiplica Gli Spazi", *Brava Casa*, September 1995, pp. 180–187.

Balint, Juliana. "Privacy Boven Intimiteit", *Eigenhuis & Interieur*, June 1992, pp. 52–57.

Balint, Juliana. "Skulptur–Huset Er Bygget Til Moblerne", *BoBedre*, N.r. 8. 1992, pp. 40–45.

Barreneche, Raul. "A Colorful Point of View", *Metropolitan Home*, June 2007, pp. 96–105.

Beaver, Robyn (ed). *100 More of the World's Best Houses*, The Images Publishing Group 2005, pp. 230–231, 264–267.

Beaver, Robyn (ed). *Another 100 of the Worlds Best Houses*, The Images Publishing Group 2003, pp. 316–319.

Beaver, Robyn (ed). *The New 100 Houses x 100 Architects*, The Images Publishing Group 2007, pp. 66–69.

Bertelson, Ann. "The Geometry of Light", *Northern California Home & Garden*, June 1991, pp. 58–67.

Biagi, Marco. "Modello al Vero", *Ville Giardini*, June 1997, pp. 10–17, cover.

Bocchino, Rafaella. "Rifare la Corte", *Ville Giardini*, April 1998, pp. 18–25.

Boekel, Andrea (ed). *50+ Vacation Homes*, The Images Publishing Group 2006, pp. 84–89.

Boekel, Andrea (ed). *Outdoor Living: Courtyards, Patios and Decks*, The Images Publishing Group 2007, pp. 10–14, 35, 72–73, 150–153, 186–189, 194–195.

Bouknight, Joanne Kellar. "Local Color Infuses a Modern Home", *The American Home*, Taunton Press 2005, pp. 19, 108–111.

Bradford, Susan. "House for Two Architects", *Builder*, October 1996, pp. 21, 65–66, 68–71, cover.

Canizares, Ana G. *San Francisco Houses*, teNeves 2003, pp. 220–253.

Carroll, Alisa. "Houses of the Spirit", *California Home + Design*, January 2007, pp. 108–115.

Castillo, Encarna. "House for Two Architects", *Maximalist Houses*, Loft Publications 2003, pp. 148–155.

Chambrun, Hervede. "Sous le Soleil de Mexico", *Maison Bricolage*, France, June 2001, pp. 66–69.

Conner, Tom. "A Retreat Far from Home", *The House to Ourselves*, Taunton Press 2004, pp. 198–207, cover.

Conner, Tom. "California Craftsman & California Modern", *Suburban Renewal*, Vicking Studio 2000, pp. 52–57, 92–97.

Dickenson, Duo. *Expressive Details*, McGraw-Hill 1996, pp. 116–121, 172–173, 212–215.

Drueding, Meghan. "Custom Home Design Awards", *Custom Home*, September/October 2003, pp. 62–63, 92–93.

Drueding, Meghan. "Custom Home Design Awards", *Custom Home*, September/October 2002, pp. 76–79.

Farnsworth, Christina. "Magical Realism", *Builder*, January 2002, pp. 186–189.

Feher, Erin. "The Light House", *California Home + Design*, March 2008, pp. 110–117.

Freeman, Allen. "Entertaining Spaces", *Architecture*, October 1989, pp. 74–75.

Fris, Anny. "Mexican Wave", *Australian House & Garden*, November 2001, pp. 138–145.

Higgins, Lisa. "Casa Not Blanca", *Metropolitan Home*, January/February 1997, pp. 78–81.

House, Cathi. "A Courtyard House in Old Mexico, Take Two", *Fine Homebuilding Houses*, Summer 2002, pp. 70–75.

House, Steven & Cathi. "A Courtyard House in Old Mexico", *Fine Homebuilding Houses*, Summer 1999, pp. 100–105.

House, Cathi & Steven. "Economical by Design", *Fine Homebuilding*, May 1994, pp. 54–57

House, Steven & Cathi. House + House Architects: *Choreographing Space*, The Images Publishing Group 1999.

House, Steven & Cathi. *Mediterranean Villages: An Architectural Journey*, The Images Publishing Group 2004.

Hutchins, Shelley. "Kitchen & Bath Studio", *Residential Architect*, November/December 2004, pp. 26–28.

Hyams, Gina. *In a Mexican Garden*, Chronicle Books 2005, pp. 18–19, cover.

Kudryavtsev, Petr. "Casa de las Estrellas", *Dom*, Russia, No. 8/61, 2004, pp. 70–79, cover.

Kudryavtsev, Petr. "Overmyer Residence", *Dom*, Russia, No. 6/59, 2004, pp. 70–79.

Lloyd, Peter. *San Francisco–A Guide to Recent Architecture*, Ellipsis London Limited-Konemann 1997, pp. 266–267, 274–275.

Lloyd, Peter. *San Francisco Houses After the Fire*, Ellipsis London Limited-Konemann 1997, p.16.

Machaz, Guiomar. "Steven E Cathi House", *Caras Decoração*, Portugal, June 1998, pp. 68–76.

Martin, Jennifer Block. "Family-Style Hillside Lair", *Better Homes & Gardens—Home*, Fall/Winter 2005, pp. 54–63.

Miller, Charles. "A Contemporary Farmhouse", *Fine Homebuilding*, September 1993, pp. 82–87.

Mizrahil, Monique. "Cubismo Americano", *Brava Casa*, Italy, April 1999, pp. 170–175.

Mizrahil, Monique. "Geometrie Naturali", *Brava Casa*, Italy, October 1996, pp. 188–193.

Porter, Paige. "Star Treatment", *Better Homes and Gardens*, May 2007, pp. 112–16.

Riquelme, Kathleen. "A San Francisco Row House", *The Studio Book*, Universe 2003, pp. 254–259.

Ritter, Joachim, "Phototime Office Laboratory & Sirius Gallery" *DBZ*, Germany, October, 1994, pp. 46–49, 50–53.

Roverselli, Elena. "Dinamismo E Luminosita", *La Mia Casa*, Italy, March 1996, pp. 52–57.

Ryder, Lee. "When Prices Bar Building a House, Remodel", *The New York Times*, October 24, 1991, C1–C6.

Saeks, Diane Dorrans. "Bold Adventure", *Phoenix Home & Garden*, February 2007, pp. 146–157.

Saekes, Diane Dorrans. "House Equals More than an Addition", *San Francisco Examiner*, July 24, 1991, pp. 1–2.

Saeks, Diane Dorrans. "Up From the Ashes", *Residential Architect*, July/August 1998, pp. 82–87.

Selover, Kelly. "Natural Mix", *House Beautiful—Kitchen & Baths*, Summer 1998, pp. 48–51, cover.

Silber, Debra Judge. "Two Styles, One Home", *Inspired House*, August 2005, pp. 56–61.

Slessor, Catherine (ed). *100 of the World's Best Houses*, The Images Publishing Group 2002, pp. 144–145.

Slessor, Catherine (ed). *Contemporary Architecture 1*, The Images Publishing Group 2003, pp. 208–211.

Sutro, Dirk. *West Coast Wave—New California Houses*, Van Nostrand Reinhold 1994, pp. 27–31.

Takahashi, Masako. *Mexican Textiles*, Chronicle Books 2003, pp. 122, 126–127.

Takahashi, Masako. *Mexicolor*, Chronicle Books 1998, pp. 124–125.

Tolliver, Jessica. "Warm & Natural", *House Beautiful—Home Building*, Spring/Summer 1999, pp. 54–59.

Toy, Maggie. *The Architect—Women in Contemporary Architecture*, The Images Publishing Group 2001, pp. 118–121.

Trelstad, Julie M. *Country Houses*, The Taunton Press Inc. 1996, pp. 60–65, 118–121.

Trucco, Terry. *Color Details and Design*, PBC International 1998, pp. 50–53, 92–95, 128–129.

Weber, Cheryl. "House + House + Island", *Residential Architect*, January/February 2001, pp. 28.

Whitely, Peter O. "Bringing in Daylight... with a Hall", *Sunset*, January, 1992, pp. 80–81.

Whitmarsh, Linda. "Cutting Edge Kitchen", *Home*, October 1993, pp. 126–129.

Project Credits

DOS IGUANAS
Client: Ed Colby & Jennifer O'Mahony
Project Size: 3,200 square feet
Location: Glen Ellen, California
Architect: Cathi House
Structural: Dominic Chu
Landscape: Topher Delaney
Contractor: Paul White Construction
Photographers: David Duncan Livingston
(1–8, 14–19, 24, 25),
Steven & Cathi House (9–13, 20–23, 26–30)

CALLE PALOMA
Client: Dr. Robert Fredericks & David Sommers
Project Size: 1,000 square feet–phase 1,
2,000 square feet–phase 2
Location: San Miguel de Allende, Mexico
Project Team: Cathi House, Rafael de la Lama
Structural: Dominic Chu, Rogelio Gomez Patlan
Landscape: Tom Sparling
Contractor: Guadalupe Gonzalez
Renderings: Rafael de la Lama
Craftspeople: Meliton Lopez (blacksmith),
Juan Carlos Padron (cabinetry)
Photographers: Steven & Cathi House

ANDERSON VALLEY
Client: Jim & Barbara Nelson
Project Size: 2,850 square feet
Location: Philo, California
Project Team: Cathi House, Michael Baushke,
Michael Tauber
Structural: Dominic Chu
Lighting: Luminella
Contractor: Innovation Builders
Renderings: Shawn Brown, Michael Baushke
Photographers: Steven & Cathi House

CASA ESTRELLAS
Client: Cathi & Steven House
Project Size: 2,000 square feet
Location: San Miguel de Allende, Mexico
Architect: Cathi House
Structural: Dominic Chu
Contractor: Guadalupe Gonzales
Craftspeople: Meliton Lopez, Transito Salazar
(blacksmiths), Francisco Caballero (cabinetry)
Rendering: Kelly Condon
Photographers: Steven House (2, 3, 5–20),
Rob Karosis (1, 4)

HARRIS PLACE
Client: Scott Kalmbach & Tjasa Owen
Project Size: 2,200 square feet
Location: San Francisco, California
Project Team: Steven House, Amena Hajjar,
Sonya Sotinsky
Structural: Dominic Chu
Interiors: Lounge Inc.
Contractor: Paul White Construction
Photographers: David Duncan Livingston
(1–10, 12), Melba Levick (11)

CASA DE BUENAS ALMAS
Client: Arthur & Carole Glaser
Project Size: 2,400 square feet
Location: Cabo Pulmo, Mexico
Architect: Cathi House
Structural: Dominic Chu
Contractor: Roberto Chamorro
Photographers: Steven & Cathi House

BUTTERNUT
Client: Boris & Irina Auerbuch
Project Size: 8,000 square feet
Location: Hillsborough, California
Project Team: Cathi House, Amena Hajjar
Structural: Dominic Chu
Landscape: Valerie Remitz & Berg Designs
Interiors: Kelly Lasser of Shelter
Contractor: Innovation Builders &
Fulwiler-James, Inc.
Photographer: David Duncan Livingston

TEABERRY LANE
Client: Spencer & Margaret Schein
Project Size: 2,300 square feet
Location: Tiburon, California
Project Team: Steven House, Sonya Sotinsky,
Emily Hodgdon
Structural: Dominic Chu
Landscape: Christine Swanson
Contractor: Robert Guild
Photographers: David Duncan Livingston
(1, 2, 4–13), Steven House (3)

CASA JOYA
Client: Steven & Iona Miller
Project Size: 2,000 square feet
Location: San Miguel de Allende, Mexico
Architect: Cathi House
Structural: Dominic Chu, Rogelio Gomez Patlan
Contractor: Guadalupe Gonzalez
Craftspeople: Meliton Lopez (blacksmith), Juan
Carlos (cabinetry)
Renderings: Cathi House (1, 2) Rafael de la
Lama (3, 4)
Photographers: Steven & Cathi House

SLEEPY HOLLOW
Project Size: 3,000 square feet
Location: Marin County, California
Project Team: Cathi House, Steven House
Structural: Dominic Chu
Landscape: Blackwelder & Associates
Interiors: Jeffers Design Group
Contractor: Summit Professional Builders
Photographers: Matthew Millman (1–19),
Steven & Cathi House (20–24)

PARROT TREE PLANTATION
Client: John Edwards
Project Size: 168 acres
Location: Roatan, Honduras
Architect: Cathi House, Sonya Sotinsky, David
Thompson, Michael Baushke
Structural: Dominic Chu
Contractor: Parrot Tree Construction
Photographers: Steven & Cathi House

MORAQUITA
Client: Tim & Susan Bratton
Project Size: 4,200 square feet
Location: Los Altos, California
Project Team: Steven House, Cathi House,
Bess Wiersema
Structural: Dominic Chu
Contractor: Fulwiler/James
Photographer: Mark Luthringer

CASA RENACIMIENTO
Client: Mayer Shacter & Susan Page
Project Size: 8,000 square feet
Location: Atotonilco, Mexico
Architect: Cathi House
Structural: Dominic Chu, Rogelio Gomez Patlan
Landscape: Timoteo Wachter
Contractor: Guadalupe Gonzalez

Craftspeople: Meliton Lopez (blacksmith),
Juan Carlos Padron (cabinetry)
Renderings: Rafael de la Lama
Photographers: Steven & Cathi House

SOUTHDOWN COURT
Client: William Wood
Project Size: 4,000 square feet
Location: Hillsborough, California
Project Team: Steven House, Cathi House, David
Thompson
Structural: Dominic Chu
Interiors: Brukoff Design Associates
Landscape: Terra Design
Contractor: Innovation Builders
Renderings: Shawn Brown
Photographer: Tom Rider

RIDGECREST
Client: David & Dianna Overmyer
Project Size: 4,400 square feet
Location: Kentfield, California
Project Team: Steven House, Amena Hajjar
Structural: Dominic Chu
Landscape: Christine Swanson
Contractor: Innovation Builders
Photographer: David Duncan Livingston

FRANCISCO MARQUEZ
Client: Tom Frye
Size: 3,200 square feet
Location: San Miguel de Allende, Mexico
Architect: Cathi House
Structural: Dominic Chu
Contractor: Guadalupe Gonzalez
Craftspeople: Meliton Lopez (blacksmith),
Francisco Caballero (cabinetry)
Photographers: Steven & Cathi House (1, 3–14),
Ricardo Vidargas (2)

CORAL SANDS
Client: John Edwards
Project Size: 18,000 square feet
Location: Roatan, Honduras
Architect: Cathi House
Structural: Dominic Chu
Renderings: Kelly Condon, Cathi House
Contractor: Parrot Tree Construction
Photographers: Steven & Cathi House

GOLDEN GATE
Client: Timothy Budziak & Ann Maurice
Project Size: 600 square feet
Location: San Francisco, California
Project Team: Steven House, Cathi House, Kelly
Condon
Interiors: Ann Maurice of Touché Design
Contractor: California Craftsmen
Photographer: David Duncan Livingston

RINCON RIDGE
Client: Eric Drucker & Linda Brownstein
Project Size: 2,200 square feet
Location: Santa Rosa, California
Project Team: Steven House, Amena Hajjar
Structural: Dominic Chu
Landscape: Christine Swanson
Contractor: Paul White Construction
Rendering: Kelly Condon
Photographer: David Duncan Livingston

PALO COLORADO
Project Size: 1,800 square feet
Location: Central Mexico
Project Team: Cathi House, Rafael de la Lama
Structural: Dominic Chu, Rogelio Gomez Patlan
Contractor: Guadalupe Gonzalez
Renderings: Rafael de la Lama
Photographers: Steven & Cathi House

Acknowledgments

We are well aware that what we do is not an individual accomplishment, but a collaborative and evolutionary one. Our clients, through their faith in our vision, with patience and perseverance, have given us opportunities to build into reality the body of work included in this monograph. It is through our clients that our work becomes more than mere dreams on paper. In most cases we only have the opportunity of working together once, every now and then twice. We would like to offer special thanks to John Edwards who we have worked with for more than 20 years in Belize and Honduras on more than a dozen projects.

We appreciate the excellent builders we have had the privilege of working with over the years. Each one brings a team of specialists and skilled workers who take our drawings and our clients' dreams into their hands and give them back as living entities. It is by their hands that this work will endure. We would especially like to thank Guadalupe Gonzales and his amazing team who have built six of the homes illustrated in these pages, as well as many others. Our work in Mexico and the pleasure of the interactions we have with the craftsmen there has added a quality to our lives that is beyond description. We are thankful every day for the fork in the road that took us there and to them.

Over the 26 years we have had this office, many talented young interns have trusted their training into our hands and have devoted themselves wholeheartedly to our projects, constantly challenging us to reach for new levels of understanding and excellence. We are proud to have shared special moments with them as they each developed into strong architects ready to stand alone.

Our families, teachers, colleagues, and friends have touched our lives in countless ways that have affected our work. We would like to thank our professors Olivio and Lucy Ferrari, Tom Regan, Gene Egger, Harold Hill, and Ellen Brattan for the questions they taught us to ask. We are indebted to the unknown architects and builders whose work has touched our souls in the course of our travels and forever changed the way we see and think, and to those like Bernard Rudofsky who helped us understand how to integrate our experiences into our work.

Very special thanks are due to Steven Lavine, Gene Egger, and Phillip Enquist for their thoughtful and insightful essays presented here. We appreciate their time and their observations, and the interactions we have shared over the years. We would also like to thank Sally Aberg, Tony Cohan, Jean Smith, and Douglas Ward for their advice and criticism on the text.

Most importantly it is through the dedicated efforts of The Images Publishing Group and their associates that our work is shared in this medium. In this age of technology where a laptop rests on every cafe table, everyone connected to the world by their fingertips, the ability to disconnect and curl up with a book, with no extraneous menu bars or pop up messages to interrupt—is a pleasure we appreciate as we look for moments of pause in our busy lives. We offer our special thanks to Paul Latham, Alessina Brooks, Beth Browne, and Rod Gilbert for their continuing efforts in keeping the medium of the book an inspiration for all of us.